Hewlett-Packard Professional Books

SNMP++: An Object-Oriented Approach to Developing Network Management Applications

Peter Erik Mellquist
Hewlett-Packard Company

To join a Prentice Hall PTR Internet
mailing list, point to:
http://www.prenhall.com/mail_lists/

Prentice Hall PTR
Upper Saddle River, NJ 07458
http://www.prenhall.com

Library of Congress Catalog-in-Publication Data

Mellquist, Peter Erik.
    SNMP++ : an object-oriented approach to developing network
management applications / Peter Erik Mellquist.
       p.   cm. -- (Hewlett-Packard professional books)
    Includes bibliographical references and index.
    ISBN 0-13-264607-2 ✓
    1. Simple Network Management Protocol Computer network protocol)
2. Object-oriented methods (Computer science) 3. C++ (Computer
program language) I. Title. II. Series.
    TK5105.583.M45   1997
    005.7'1--dc21   97-25878
                                            CIP

Editorial / production supervision and interior formatting: **Vanessa Moore**
Cover design director: **Jerry Votta**
Cover design: **Marita Froimson**
Manufacturing manager: **Alan Fischer**
Acquisitions editor: **Bernard M. Goodwin**
Marketing manager: **Miles Williams**
Manager, Hewlett-Packard Press: **Patricia Pekary**

Published by Prentice-Hall, Inc.
A Simon & Schuster Company
Upper Saddle River, NJ 07458

Prentice Hall books are widely used by corporations and government
agencies for training, marketing, and resale.

The publisher offers discounts on this book when ordered in bulk
quantities. For more information, contact Corporate Sales Department,
Phone: 800-382-3419, Fax: 201-236-7141, Email: corpsales@prenhall.com

or write: Prentice Hall PTR
               Corporate Sales Department
               One Lake Street
               Upper Saddle River, NJ 07458

Printed in the United States of America

10   9   8   7   6   5   4   3   2   1

ISBN 0-13-264607-2

Prentice-Hall International (UK) Limited, *London*
Prentice-Hall of Australia Pty. Limited, *Sydney*
Prentice-Hall of Canada, Inc., *Toronto*
Prentice-Hall Hispanoamericana S.A., *Mexico*
Prentice-Hall of India Private Limited, *New Delhi*
Prentice-Hall of Japan, Inc., *Tokyo*
Simon & Schuster Asia Pte. Ltd., *Singapore*
Editora Prentice-Hall do Brasil, Ltda., *Rio de Janeiro*

Table of Contents

v

List of Tables

List of Figures

List of Examples

Preface

$\mathbf{T}$his book presents an object-oriented approach to developing network management applications using the Simple Network Protocol and C++. Developed by Hewlett-Packard Company, a leader in network management technology, SNMP++ has been successfully utilized in a number of commercial products. Unlike other books on SNMP that focus on lower-level mechanisms of network management, the focus of this book is upon real product development using the experience of many engineers, network managers, and network professionals. This book will show you how object-oriented concepts are applied to the development of network management applications from analysis, through design, to implementation.

In order to meet the challenge of the explosive growth in networked computing, powerful new tools are required to allow management of larger and more complex systems in a timely manner. Object-oriented tools provide many of the benefits needed to meet this challenge. Up to now, network management development has been a cumbersome task requiring the expertise of many valuable resources. SNMP++ brings the object-oriented advantage to network management development and in doing so allows you to develop powerful applications as never before.

There are a variety of Simple Network Management Protocol (SNMP) Application Programmer Interfaces (APIs) that exist for the creation of management applications. The majority of these provide a large library of functions that require the programmer to be familiar with the inner workings of SNMP and network management. Most of these APIs are platform-specific, resulting in SNMP code specific to an operating system platform and thus not portable. Application development using C++ has entered the mainstream and, with it, a rich set of reusable class libraries are now readily available. What has been missing is a standard set of C++ classes for system and network management development. SNMP++, a reusable C++ class library, offers power and flexibility that would otherwise be difficult to implement and manage. An object-oriented approach to SNMP network programming provides many benefits, including the following.

Platform Portability

SNMP++ is a portable Application Programmer Interface (API). A major goal of SNMP++ is to provide portability across a variety of operating systems, network operating systems, and network management platforms. SNMP code developed using SNMP++ will port to other operating system platforms without any changes. For most developers, more platforms mean broader market coverage. Broader market coverage means more revenue. SNMP++ makes this possible with minimal effort. SNMP++ has currently been ported for Microsoft Windows NT, Windows 95, and a variety of UNIX platforms.

Network Management Developer Power

SNMP++ provides power that would otherwise be difficult to implement and manage. Utilizing object orientation, SNMP++ allows powerful applications to be constructed with minimal coding effort. Powerful features of SNMP++ include automatic SNMP resource and memory management, and an automatic bilingual SNMP interface (the ability to manage SNMP version 1 and version 2 agents through the same API). Together, these features provide the developer with a powerful set of tools and create the framework for network management application development.

Putting the Simple Back into SNMP

An object-oriented approach to SNMP programming should be easy to use. After all, this is supposed to be a *simple* network management protocol. SNMP++ puts the *simple* back into SNMP! An object-oriented approach to SNMP encapsulates and hides the internal mechanisms of SNMP and in doing so allows you to focus on your application. In order to use SNMP++, you don't have to be an expert in C++. Only a minimal understanding of C++ basics is required. Similarly, you don't have to be an expert in the lower-level details of SNMP and network management.

Programming Safety

Most SNMP APIs require the programmer to manage a variety of computing resources. These include low-level SNMP data structures and network layer transports. SNMP++ provides safety by managing these resources internally. By realizing the benefits of a safe, robust API, you can stay focused on your application development and not waste time chasing memory leaks that are due to a difficul- to-use API.

Programming Extensibility

A central theme to object orientation is that of programming exten-sibility. SNMP++ is designed to be extended easily. Extensions to SNMP++ include supporting new operating systems, network protocols, network management platforms, new versions of SNMP, and adding new application-specific features tailored to your specific needs. Through C++ class derivation, users of SNMP++ can inherit what they like and over-load what they wish to redefine.

Rapid Application Development

SNMP++ addresses one of the most important issues in software development—how to deliver quality products in a timely manner. SNMP++ is a reusable technology that has allowed products to be suc-cessful and reach markets in a timely manner.

GUIDE TO READERS

This book is organized into three parts. Each part may be read separately, out of order, or if you are already familiar with the topics found in the part, not at all. The book utilizes a large number of examples including a fully implemented SNMP browser, which can be found on the accompanying CD-ROM.

Part I: An Introduction to Network Management and SNMP++   Part I focuses on the background of network management, including the objectives, business, technologies, and standards associated with management. A special emphasis is provided on the Simple Network Management Protocol (SNMP), its history, and current status. For those readers who are already well familiar with SNMP and its details, this part can be skipped. Additionally, this part provides a chapter on object orientation and C++, covering the concepts that directly apply to SNMP++.

Part II: The SNMP++ Framework   Part II defines the set of classes that make up the SNMP++ framework. SNMP++ is comprised of a set of C++ classes that collectively provide a framework for the development of network management applications. Each class is defined and a variety of examples are given. This part may be utilized as a language reference for SNMP++.

Part III: Developing Network Management Applications   This last part focuses on the construction of a complete network management application using Microsoft Windows Visual C++ (MSVC++). A complete SNMP browser application would include support of SNMP version 1 and version 2 agents. The full source code for the examples is provided on the accompanying CD-ROM. The example program runs on both Microsoft Windows NT and Microsoft Windows 95.

THE SCOPE OF THIS BOOK

The topics found within this book focus primarily on the Network Management Station (NMS) side of network management. This is in contrast to the embedded systems side where SNMP agents are embedded within devices. Many of the concepts described are universal to SNMP, including managers and agents. There are a variety of books on the market that focus on the esoteric details of SNMP and network management. This book differs in that it focuses primarily on building complete network management solutions using a technology that is well developed and successfully deployed.

The process and methodology required to build network management solutions are not straightforward. Much of the documentation and design material regarding network management and SNMP exist in the form of Internet Engineering Task Force (IETF) Requests For Comments (RFCs), a form not easily deciphered by many. This book presents this information on an "as-needed" basis. That is, rather than describe all the RFCs and their content, only the elements that apply to SNMP++ are described.

ACKNOWLEDGEMENTS

SNMP++ would have never been created without the vision and effort of Kim Banker. Special thanks are given to a few project managers who saw value in this technology, including Bob McGuire, Lloyd Serra, Moises Medina, and Harry Feit. Bob Natale and the WinSNMP group have provided the forum where SNMP++ has been discussed and developed over the Internet.

Part I:
An Introduction to Network
Management and SNMP++

CHAPTER 1

Systems and Network Management

Network management is the ability to monitor, control, and plan the resources and components of computer systems and networks. It is clear that this is not an easy task and is one that cannot be accomplished effectively by using manual techniques alone. Computer networks save time and money; unfortunately they also take time and money to operate. System and network management attempts to use the power of computers and networks to manage systems and networks themselves. In doing so, network managers rely on a variety of tools. As we approach the time of a computer on every desktop, we also rely more and more on system and network management as the means to ensure that everything operates and provides reliable service. Systems and network management is not only important, it is a big business. The chart in Figure 1.1 on the next page shows the market size estimates for system and network management services. By the year 2000, the total systems and network management business is estimated to grow to $4.3B [Dataquest].

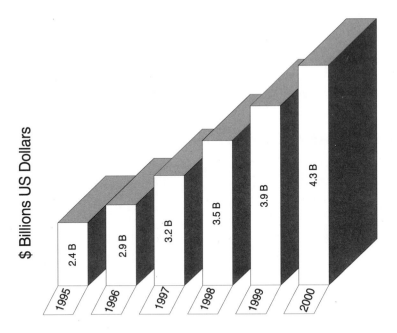

Figure 1.1   Estimated Systems and Network Management Market.

Once while visiting a customer site, I met a network manager who worked for a large stock brokerage firm. The network manager explained to me how important it was to keep his network up and running and how he was interested in any and all tools that could help him do so. He also explained that he would be rewarded with a yearly $20,000 bonus if he could minimize his network downtime to less than one hour a month! Not all networks are so mission-critical, but all networks require some degree of management. System management typically relies on tools for software inventory, software distribution, and computer virus checking. Network management tends to focus more on device management, traffic management, planning, and security. The focus of this book is on the development of management tools that utilize the Simple Network Management Protocol (SNMP) for systems and network management. There are various management protocols and standards I will present in this chapter that have applications in system and network management. Of these, SNMP is by far the most popular.

MANAGEMENT OF SYSTEMS AND NETWORKS

Like much in the computer information age, network management is a problem created by computers. Computers are only supposed to solve problems and steal jobs, right? Here is a place where computers have solved one problem and created another. In fact, here is an instance where a whole industry has arisen simply for systems and network management. No matter how you look at it, network management is necessary to keep networks up and running. Without network management very little would be possible—routers would cease to work, traffic levels would saturate networks, hackers would violate fire walls, and, worst of all, users would not tolerate it. Computers can do many things better than people can and one of them is to provide automation for the management of critical system and network resources.

What about "self-managed" or "manage-less" systems and networks? Even though this type of management may not require a full-time expert, management processes still must run automatically and the technology that makes it happen is much the same as in human-managed systems. We may be able to reduce the amount of human effort it takes to manage networks, but it is clear that we will not be able to remove management technology itself. In order to minimize human intervention, new and powerful tools are required.

Architecture of Management

Central to the theme of network management are the concepts of a *manager* and an *agent*. (See Figure 1.2 on the next page.) At least one network host found within a managed network is designated the *manager* or *Network Management Station* (NMS). The responsibility of the NMS is to monitor and control the *agents*. An *agent* is a software component residing in a networked appliance that is responsible for monitoring and controlling the environment in which it operates. This includes just about any device with a network interface that can be reached by the NMS. Typically, the *manager* issues a request to an *agent* and the *agent* responds with the appropriate information. In this manner, a single NMS can manage a variety of *agents*.

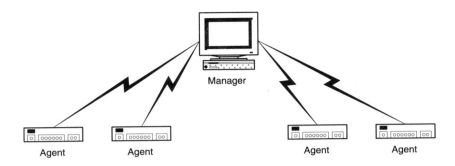

Figure 1.2   Manager and Agents.

Network management can be implemented utilizing various architectures based on their type and size. Basically, there are two architectures that can be used, *centralized management* and *distributed management*. Centralized management enables the centralization of management control and responsibility in one location. This is ideal for systems that are limited in size or geographically isolated. Distributed management enables the distribution of management control and responsibility. Distributed architectures provide management for large, geographically distributed systems and are also beneficial when critical network resources must be conserved, such as Wide Area Network (WAN) links. SNMP and SNMP++ are utilized for the development of both centralized and distributed management systems.

Centralized Management   A centralized architecture relies on information and control to exist at a single centralized location. This simplifies the management of networks that are not large in size. Networks that are not geographically distributed can be managed effectively using this management model. Since monitoring and control reside at a single point, a network manager must also reside at the same point. In order to monitor the networks actively, a centralized management station must poll or query network devices found within each network. This introduces management traffic on the internetwork connections. See Figure 1.3.

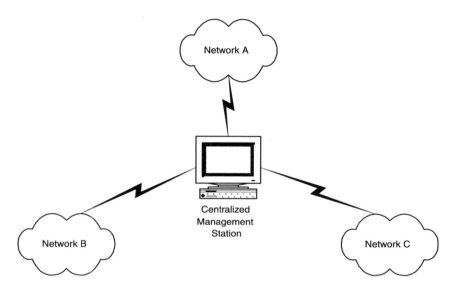

Figure 1.3   Centralized Management System.

Distributed Management   In contrast to a centralized model, a distributed model distributes information and control such that each network or geographically distributed site is responsible for itself. In a distributed model, management is pushed down to its lowest level. In this model, we have mid-level managers that are responsible for their own domain of management. Important information that is pertinent to the entire internetwork is forwarded to a manager-of-managers. (See Figure 1.4. on the next page.) This model scales well for networks that are large in size.

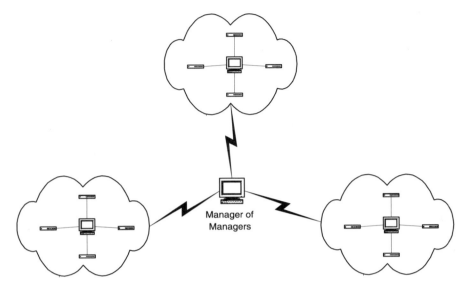

Figure 1.4   Distributed Management.

GOALS OF MANAGEMENT

One might ask, "Why is network management so important? Why can't I just put together a network and let it run?" There must be some compelling reason why network management is required. As organizations continue to automate and invest in network infrastructure, the need for and cost of management become predominant. That is, the initial costs of computers, routers, hubs, and printers are a fraction of the cost that will be incurred to maintain and keep them running over their lifetime. Manageability, therefore, is a major influence factor when these systems are designed, selected, and purchased. The maintenance of a networked system involves highly skilled and salaried people. System and network management, from a developer's perspective, is about devising solutions that reduce the cost of ownership and operation. In order to make this possible, we must turn to technologies that enable us to address this need easily.

Keeping Networks Running

Minimally, systems and networks must be operational, or remain up and running. This says nothing about the quality of service or the difficulties one may have using the network. There are times when a network just will not work. The ability to detect or prevent such scenarios is crucial to a network manager. SNMP is a vital tool for monitoring and gathering information on a network's health. Without SNMP, it would not be possible to compute a simple metric such as how long a network has been up and running.

Maintaining Network Performance

Simply maintaining an operational network is not sufficient. A network must also perform at some minimally acceptable level of quality. When will users start to become dissatisfied? A major responsibility of network management is to provide an acceptable level of performance level, or Quality Of Service (QOS). If a performance problem exists, it must be pinpointed and resolved in a timely manner. SNMP plays a vital role in performance monitoring. Using SNMP, vital network traffic statistics may be remotely acquired and analyzed. This information can be used for both short- and long-term analysis. Short-term analysis allows for the rapid detection and resolution of faults and problems. Longer-term trend analysis allows for the detection of problems that manifest themselves gradually and also provides valuable information for network growth.

Reducing the Cost of Ownership

Simply purchasing network equipment and installing it is quite inexpensive compared to the longer-term cost of managing and maintaining it. Network management can be divided into two main categories, *reactive* and *proactive* management. In terms of the reduction of ownership costs, reactive management is much more expensive. This is true because when a network fails, it frequently needs to be fixed immediately and at any cost. While fault and performance management are important, they are primarily used in a reactive manner. When there is a fault in a system, you react to it by identifying the problem and eliminating it.

When performance reaches an unacceptable level, you react to it by finding the source of the problem and fixing it. While *reactive* management is required, *proactive* management keeps these problems from happening in the first place. In doing so, proactive management promotes the reduction of ownership costs. Proactive management allows a network to be properly planned and built, thus avoiding expensive crisis scenarios. This can be something as simple as running redundant cable when a network is wired, or it can mean trending long-term performance data to look for gradual changes in network traffic patterns. This allows for answering questions such as "Has network utilization increased in the last month?" or "Is response time getting better or worse?" Clearly, management is required in order to reduce the cost of ownership.

MANAGEMENT STANDARDS AND PROTOCOLS

Standards play a critical role in the management of systems and networks. Standards allow heterogeneous systems to be managed using a single technology. Without standards, systems would have to be managed with protocols specific to each vendor or manufacturer of a network component. Standards are both good and bad. They are good in that they ensure interoperability between different components of a system. They can be bad when standards bodies, which oversee the creation of standards, fail to deliver on features required by the networking community. This often results in non-standard proprietary technologies.

Networking Standards Organizations

There are a few standard bodies that oversee system and network management standards. These bodies differ in the domains of standardization they attempt to address and the processes they utilize to achieve a single, agreed-upon set of goals.

Internet Engineering Task Force (IETF)   The most successful work in the area of standardized network management technologies has come from the Internet Engineering Task Force (IETF). Along with many other protocol standards, the IETF is responsible for the creation of SNMP. The IETF is an organization in which anyone can participate by attending meetings or by using electronic mail. The Internet Engineering

Task Force is a subbody of the Internet Architectural Board (IAB). Together with the Internet Research Task Force (IRTF), they form both short- and long-term task forces with networking protocols and Internet standards in mind. The IETF is responsible for short-term engineering tasks and standard proposals; the IRTF is responsible for longer-term research efforts. Each of these bodies, the IETF and IRTF, are managed by steering groups. The IETF is managed by the Internet Engineering Steering Group (IESG) and the IRTF is managed by the Internet Research Steering Group (IRSG). As described above, the IETF may seem like a big bureaucratic organization. In contrast to other standard organizations, the IETF has proven itself by accomplishing a great deal in a timely manner. The IETF is comprised of a Chair of the IETF and directors of functional areas. Within each area, working groups are designated to complete specific tasks. For example, within the network management functional area can be found a variety of working groups pertaining to network management tasks.

Each working group has a charter and, if successful, produces a set of documents. These documents are called *Internet-Drafts*. When published the draft may be categorized as *Standards Track, Experimental,* or *Informational*. Standards track drafts follow the order of *Proposed-Draft, Draft,* or *Standard*. Not all *Internet-Drafts* make it to full *Standard*. As enhancements to existing drafts are made, some drafts end up as *Obsolete* or *Historic*. Each draft created is given a Request For Comment (RFC) number and is made available through an electronic archive. A list of all RFCs published can be found at *http://www.ietf.org*. Anyone is free to design and build a protocol for use in the Internet suite provided that it is documented in the form of an RFC.

Another important standards body is the Internet Assigned Numbers Authority (IANA), which is responsible for keeping and assigning lists of values used in the Internet protocol suite. For example, the TCP/IP port number 161 is the assigned Internet Protocol port for SNMP protocol requests. All of the specifications regarding SNMP and its related components are represented as IETF RFCs. This includes the actual SNMP protocol, as well as a wide variety of Management Information Base (MIB) definitions. The components for the SNMP framework are defined in the set of RFCs [SNMP RFCs] shown in Table 1.1 on the next page.

Table 1.1   SNMP Requests For Comments (RFCs).

RFC #	Name
1901	Introduction to Community-based SNMPv2
1902	SMI for SNMPv2
1903	Textual Conventions for SNMPv2
1904	Conformance Statements for SNMPv2
1905	Protocol Operations for SNMPv2
1906	Transport Mappings for SNMPv2
1907	MIB for SNMPv2
1908	Coexistence between SNMPv1 and SNMPv2

De Facto Standards Groups   In addition to formal standards bodies, de facto or universally accepted standards that originated from a nonstandard body also play a vital role in network management. The most notable de facto standard body for system management is the Desktop Management Task Force (DMTF) [DMTF]. The DMTF is a group of companies with a common interest in providing standard mechanisms for the management of desktop computers and peripherals. The DMTF has produced the Desktop Management Interface (DMI), which enables the instrumentation and access of desktop system information, including personal computers (PCs), file servers, and printers. Unlike the more formal and democratic IETF, the DMTF is controlled and run by a few core companies. The DMTF addresses many issues not dealt with by the IETF, such as a standard management API.

Standardized Management Protocols

Simple Network Management Protocol (SNMP)   SNMP is by far the most popular system and network management protocol. More devices and systems are managed with SNMP than with any other management protocol. This is true largely because SNMP is quite small and inexpensive to deploy. That is, it can be implemented in devices with minimal memory and CPU resources. This is in contrast to the Open Systems Interconnection (OSI) management protocols, which are complex and thus more expensive to deploy. SNMP was developed to provide a basic, easy-to-implement network management tool for the Transport Control Protocol/Internet Protocol (TCP/IP) suite of protocols. This includes a framework of operation and a representation of management information within the framework. The Structure of Management Information (SMI) allows for the definition of Management Information Bases (MIBs). MIBs are analogous to database schemas, for those familiar with database definitions. A managed entity, also known as an agent, includes one or more MIBs that define what information is manageable. This includes a standard set of management information resources that are part of the SNMP framework, as well as vendor-specific management information that enables a vendor to instrument the specifics of the device. The ability to define a custom MIB allows SNMP management to be extended to meet a particular need of a vendor's device.

Common Management Information Protocol (CMIP) SNMP is not the only network management protocol. The International Organization for Standardization (ISO) and the International Consultative Committee on Telegraphy and Telephony (CCITT) have worked together to create a network management standard for the Open Systems Interconnection (OSI) environment. The result is the Common Management Information Service (CMIS) and the Common Management Information Protocol (CMIP), which implements CMIS. The OSI systems management standard is a large and complex one. It is this complexity and size that largely motivated the creation of a more simple scheme, SNMP. Nevertheless, CMIS and CMIP have found usage in the telecommunications industry [CMIP].

Desktop Management Interface (DMI) The Desktop Management Interface (DMI) was developed by the Desktop Management Task Force (DMTF), an incorporation of companies with an interest in providing a mechanism to manage the components of a desktop. DMI acts as an abstraction between management software and the components that must be managed. DMI can be used to manage components locally, no network, or remotely using Remote Procedure Calls (RPCs). DMI can be mapped to existing protocols such as SNMP or CMIP. Where CMIP and SNMP use MIBs, DMI uses Managed Information Format (MIF) files to describe managed components. When new components are added to a system, new corresponding MIFs are added. This provides an extensible mechanism to manage a system as new hardware and software components are introduced [DMI].

AREAS OF NETWORK MANAGEMENT

Network management can be broken down into five functional areas. Each area defines a discrete domain of management with specific needs. Depending on the network to be managed, a specific area may be emphasized or de-emphasized.

Fault Management

Fault management is concerned with the detection, isolation, and correction of fault conditions in a network. This can be accomplished using both reactive and proactive forms of management, although it is mostly accomplished today using reactive methods. Through active monitoring and event notification, fault conditions can be detected, isolated, and remedied. Active monitoring is achieved by polling for information from managed components. (See Figure 1.5.) When the information retrieved exceeds some predetermined threshold, a fault condition can be detected. Although polling can be effective, it requires network bandwidth that is then wasted when no faults are present. Polling also becomes difficult when dealing with a large network where many components need to be queried.

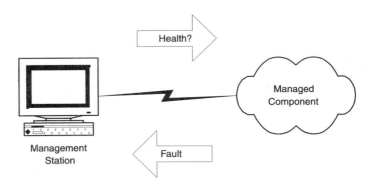

Figure 1.5   Fault Detection via Polling.

An alternate approach to polling is event notification. Event notification enables a networked agent to notify a manager in the event a fault has occurred. (See Figure 1.6.) This saves network bandwidth since communication occurs only when a fault is present. Event notification by itself may not catch all errors because when a network component crashes, it may not have the opportunity to notify someone.

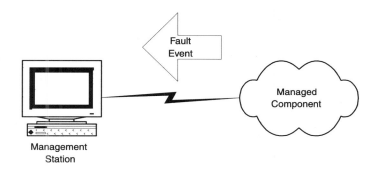

Figure 1.6   Fault Detection via Event Notification.

The solution is to mix both approaches and have low frequency polling with event notification. In the event a networked component dies without notifying someone, the low-frequency poll cycle will report the error. Since polling is performed only at a low frequency, unnecessary network traffic is not introduced. In the event a notification is received, the polling frequency for that managed component may be increased. This technique is also known as notification-based polling.

Accounting Management

Accounting management is concerned with the allocation of resources within a networked system and charging for their services. This type of management includes the collection of usage information from networked components and the creation of accurate billing information. Today, many Internet Service Providers (ISPs) use this form of management to determine how much to bill clients who use their Internet services. Accounting management is typically performed as a low-priority task while other management tasks such as fault management take precedence. As more and more people become connected to the Internet and share key network resources, accounting management will come to play a bigger role.

Another important area of accounting management is asset management and the inventory of networked components. This enables the automatic creation of inventory lists of networked equipment. When dealing with large systems, this can be particularly useful.

Configuration Management

Configuration management deals with updating, changing, and modifying resources within the network. Configuration of networked components is primarily performed when the component is first installed. Configuration also may be a result of fault management where faults are corrected through configuration changes. Through configuration, specific components of a network may be gracefully shut down or turned on. Since configuration may change the attributes and behavior of a device, secure configuration is of primary concern.

Performance Management

Performance management is concerned with the analysis and evaluation of system and network performance. Performance management is an important area of management in which both short- and long-term performance can be evaluated. Short-term analysis of performance data may determine immediately noticeable conditions, while longer-term analysis helps to shed light on conditions that happen slowly over time.

Security Management

Security management provides for the protection of resources within a system or network. Security becomes more important with increased connectivity. Security management is closely related to fault and configuration management since configuration of important devices must be secure. Security management can be divided into two areas: management of the security of a network and management using secure protocols. Management of the security of a network includes managing and configuring passwords on servers so that unauthorized access is prohibited. Management using secure protocols includes making sure that management of agents is performed using protocols that prevent unauthenticated access.

CHAPTER 2

Introduction to the Simple Network Management Protocol

The Simple Network Management Protocol (SNMP) was developed to provide a basic, easy-to-implement network management tool for the Transport Control Protocol/Internet Protocol (TCP/IP) suite of protocols. SNMP is more than just a protocol. It is a collection of specifications, Internet Engineering Task Force Request for Comments (IETF RFCs), that are used for network management. SNMP includes the actual protocol, the definition of managed information, and other related components. The SNMP management model is based on the notion of an SNMP *manager* and an SNMP *agent*—where an agent is "managed" by a manager. (See Figure 2.1 on the next page.) Agents typically instrument components in a network or system and provide this information to a manager that requests the information. The simpleness of SNMP is mostly appreciated by these agents, which frequently have limited computing resources.

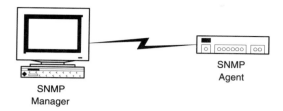

Figure 2.1   SNMP Manager and Agent.

BRIEF HISTORY OF SNMP

In the early days of TCP/IP, there was little effort or consideration given to the design or development of network management. Of the few tools available, the Internet Control Message Protocol (ICMP) offered some very simple management capability. Using ICMP Ping, the networking interface portion of a TCP/IP machine can be verified as up-and-running, and basic response times can be computed. Although Ping worked and continues to work well, it has very limited functionality. Specifically, one can not acquire information from the network entity in question. And, if information can be accessed, there is no standard way to move the information to the manager who then must be able to interpret the data and do something with it.

In order to address such network management needs, a few proposals emerged, including the Simple Network Management Protocol (SNMP). In the beginning, SNMP was an enhanced version of the Simple Monitoring Gateway Protocol (SGMP) [SGMP]. As different proposals were developed and reviewed, the Internet Advisory Board (IAB) approved SNMP as a short-term solution and categorized the preferred Common Management Information Protocol (CMIP), also known as CMOT over TCP/IP as the longer-term solution. At that time, it was thought that the TCP/IP protocol suite would migrate to the OSI-based protocols within some reasonable time frame. This did not happen and it now seems highly unlikely ever to happen! In order to meet the needs of network management, SNMP can be developed quickly and thereby provide a feasible solution. To enable the convergence of SNMP and CMOT, the IAB dictated that both protocols use the identical database definition syntax for managed information. This would allow a single set of management information to be defined for both protocols. This intention was good because much effort goes into the design and definition of managed information. It was soon discovered, however, that the management information required by CMOT would be overly complex for SNMP. CMOT, therefore, would increase overhead and reduce the simplicity of SNMP. The IAB agreed that this was undesirable. After that, SNMP and CMOT had very little in common.

SNMP was implemented quickly in a variety of managed entities. All of these devices implemented the common set of SNMP management information and protocols and thereby allowed heterogeneous networks and systems to be managed. Today we have a wide variety of devices that utilize the SNMP management framework for network and system management, and the number continues to grow everyday.

THE SNMP AGENT

The SNMP agent, or simply agent, consists of a software process that responds to SNMP protocol requests by an SNMP manager. Agents have been developed to instrument networking devices such as personal computers (PCs), workstations, network repeaters, routers, switches, and just about every kind of network appliance that requires management. SNMP agents also may be utilized to instrument software processes. Since the SNMP agent is a piece of software, it requires an operating system platform on which to operate. This platform in turn requires some sort of network transport services by which the agent can interact with a manager. SNMP is designed to operate over a variety of network transport protocols, including the Transport Control Protocol/Internet Protocol (TCP/IP) and Novell's Internet Packet Exchange (IPX). SNMP agents can exist, therefore, in either of these environments.

SNMP agents can be utilized in two basic roles, monitoring and control. An agent operating in a monitoring role may monitor hardware or software. When an SNMP manager requests monitored information, the agent responds either by returning stored monitored data or by querying the hardware or software to be monitored. Monitoring is a passive action in that a manager requesting information can do no harm to the agent because monitoring is a read-only operation. Monitoring agents are useful for returning status and performance information. For example, with an SNMP monitoring agent one can determine what options are configured on a device or how many errors have occurred over some period of time. Since monitoring in itself can do no harm, security is not a primary concern.

The other type of role an agent can play is that of control. A control SNMP agent can directly control hardware or software to which it is connected. This enables an SNMP manager to remotely control some hardware or software by issuing SNMP requests to the agent. Because control is nonpassive operation, it alters information and behavior, and thus security is an issue. Without secure access anyone can control the device in which the agent resides. For this reason, an agent that operates in a control context should be used more judiciously in environments where security is an issue.

One special type of role an SNMP agent may play is that of a proxy agent. A proxy agent, as its name implies, carries out proxy requests to some other non-SNMP protocol entity. These requests are translated on-the-fly by the proxy agent and appear to the manager as any other SNMP request. For example, consider an SNMP agent operating on a PC. The agent instruments a variety of network information regarding the PC's connectivity. In addition, the PC has a Redundant Power Supply (RPS) connected to it that supports a proprietary (non-SNMP) protocol. Operating in a proxy role, the SNMP agent makes the RPS protocol appear just like the SNMP protocol. The benefit of using proxy agents is that non-SNMP protocols do not need to be re-implemented using SNMP. And all management can be conducted using only SNMP.

Figure 2.2 shows the SNMP agent and all its roles.

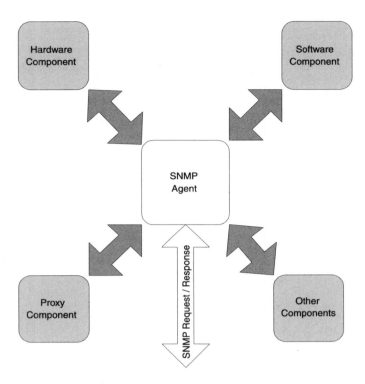

Figure 2.2   SNMP Agent.

An agent can be broken down into three main components: the protocol engine; the Management Information Base (MIB), and the Instrumentation Layer (IL), which interfaces a managed device's equipment to be monitored to the MIB. All information accessible through the agent is viewed as part of the agent's MIB. When reading or writing information to an agent, MIB objects are therefore referenced. See Figure 2.3 on the next page.

By reading information from an agent's MIB, an SNMP manager can monitor the agent. By writing or altering information, an SNMP manager can control the behavior of the managed entity on which the agent resides. Together, monitoring and control enable an SNMP manager to provide network management effectively.

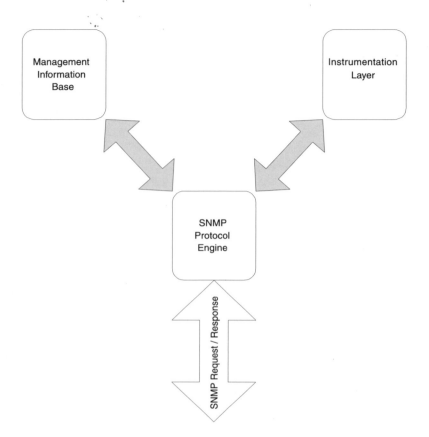

Figure 2.3   Components of an SNMP Agent.

Agent SNMP Protocol Engine

An agent's protocol engine is responsible for processing SNMP requests from an SNMP manager. This includes receiving the request, decoding it, servicing the requested information, and sending the response back to the manager. The SNMP standard requires that SNMP requests and responses be issued on connectionless transports. For the TCP/IP suite of protocols, the User Datagram Protocol (UDP) is used. It is worth mentioning that connectionless transports are unreliable. This means that the protocol itself does nothing to compensate for the inherent unreliability of network communication. Using unreliable connectionless protocols, one can be subjected to lost datagrams, reordered datagrams, and duplicate datagrams. An SNMP management architecture must take this into account and compensate for these deficiencies. So why use a connectionless protocol like UDP for SNMP? Why not use the reliable TCP protocol instead? Since one of the initial design goals of SNMP was to keep things simple and easy to implement, connectionless protocols were chosen. UDP is smaller and easier to implement in devices with limited memory resources. Furthermore, the expense of setting up and tearing down TCP connections for each SNMP request was thought to be detrimental to performance.

Management Information Base

One of the most important concepts in SNMP management is that of an agent's Management Information Base (MIB). The MIB is the view of management information that an agent exports to an SNMP manager. All information accessed or modified through the agent is accessed or modified through the MIB. For example, in order to read a value from an agent, an SNMP manager queries the agent's MIB. In order to write a value, the SNMP manager writes to the MIB. The MIB is comprised of *managed objects* that each have a unique identifier. It is worth pointing out that although the components of the MIB are called *objects*, they are not object-oriented in any way. Instead think of each managed object as a database record that has a unique identifier and a value.

Each managed object has a unique identifier, called an MIB *object identifier*. To reference an MIB object, the object identifier must be used. All SNMP standard agents are required to support a standard set of *managed objects*. This enables an SNMP manager to access the MIB objects through a standard set of object identifiers. For every MIB object there exists an MIB definition that defines the managed object. The definition covers a variety of attributes, including the object identifier, the syntax type, access permissions, description, and instance information. MIB definitions are created using a special syntax called Abstract Syntax Notation One (ASN.1). ASN.1 is a machine-independent data description that was initially developed for use in the OSI suite of protocols. For SNMP, only a subset of ASN.1 is used. The rules for writing MIB definitions using ASN.1 are defined in the Structure of Management

Information (SMI), a part of the SNMP RFCs. Example 2.1 shows the definition of an MIB object, `myMibObject`, which is a 32-bit integer. It can take on values from one to ten, has read and write permissions, and is accessable through the object identifier `myObjects.1`.

Example 2.1   An SNMP Managed Object Defined in ASN.1.

```
myMibObject OBJECT-TYPE
    SYNTAX        Integer32 (1..10)
    MAX-ACCESS    read-write
    STATUS        current
    DESCRIPTION
       "An example MIB object"
    ::= { myObjects 1 }
```

When MIBs for vendor-specific agents are defined, they usually extend existing standardized MIBs. A customized SNMP agent's MIB then becomes a set of standardized MIB objects, plus a set of vendor-specific MIB objects. Together they form a customized SNMP agent for a particular management need. Table 2.1 shows a set of standardized MIB definitions and their descriptions.

Table 2.1   A Few Popular MIB Definitions.

RFC #	Name
1315	Frame Relay MIB
1516	IEEE 802.3 Repeater MIB
1659	RS-232 MIB
1660	Parallel Printer Interface MIB
1669	Modem MIB
1695	ATM MIB
1697	Relational Database System MIB
1757	Remote Monitoring MIB
1759	Printer MIB

MIB Compilers   Since an MIB definition is in the form of ASN.1 syntax, a different form of the MIB is required that can be embedded in a managed agent. In order to utilize an MIB definition and to generate the code and data that make up the embedded MIB, an MIB compiler is required. (See Figure 2.4.) An MIB compiler is an important tool that can work on ASN.1 MIB definitions in a variety of ways, including:

- **Check the syntax of an MIB definition.**   When you develop a custom MIB, an MIB compiler can be useful to help you find ASN.1 syntax errors in the definition. When complete and correct, the MIB definition then can be interpreted by anyone familiar with MIB definitions.

- **Generate source code for use in an agent.**   Once an MIB definition has been developed, you can use it to generate source code to be used in the development of an SNMP agent. The MIB compiler generates source code "stubs" that the agent developer must complete.

- **Generate code for use in a manager.**   Once an MIB definition and an agent have been developed, the MIB definition can be used to construct a manager application that references the MIB objects. A management application may use this information in a variety of ways.

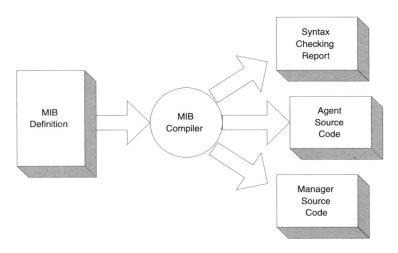

Figure 2.4   MIB Compiler.

The ability to easily extend an MIB with vendor-specific objects is an important capability. Vendor-specific MIB extensions are managed through the Internet Authority Numbers Association (IANA), which designates vendor-specific MIB object identifiers. This ensures that vendor-specific object identifiers do not clash.

Management applications are required to be aware of MIB-to-agent relationships so that, given an agent, a manager will know what managed objects exist. For example, when dealing with a networked laser printer with an SNMP agent and a standard printer MIB, an SNMP manager is required to know which managed objects exist. This requires that the SNMP management application have knowledge about the standard printer MIB.

Instrumentation Layer

In order to populate an MIB with management information, data must be monitored and placed in it. With the aid of an MIB compiler, an MIB definition can be used to generate the instrumentation stub routines. The stub routines are computer-generated code that is called whenever a particular management object is accessed. The details for each stub must be provided with actual code by the agent implementor. Each managed object on the agent can therefore have its own piece of code invoked whenever the MIB object is referenced.

THE SNMP MANAGER

An SNMP Manager is responsible for accessing, modifying, or receiving information from managed agents. Managers, like agents, come in many flavors. A manager and agent may cooperatively reside on the same managed entity. If this is the case, the entity is called a "dual role entity." Managers are typically responsible for managing a set or a domain of agents. There are many applications that utilize management information, including management platforms and stand-alone applications. Like the agent developer, a manager developer uses an MIB definition to determine what information an agent has and what it represents. See Figure 2.5.

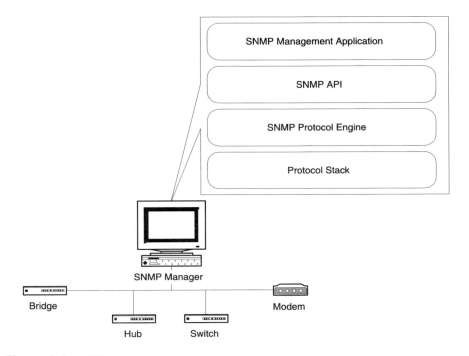

Figure 2.5 SNMP Manager.

Management Platform

A management platform provides a platform for the management of heterogeneous devices. In order to do so, the platform provides a number of services, including the automatic discovery of SNMP devices, the display of the devices on a map, the ability to browse the device using an SNMP browser, and provision of an Application Programmers Interface (API) to enable management applications to be developed for vendor-specific devices. The last area, the API, is crucial to a platform's success. In order for a management platform to be successful, it must provide an easy way for a vendor's devices to be well-managed within the platform. SNMP++ has been designed from the ground up with this in mind. SNMP++ has a number of features that provide for clean platform integration, enabling developers to seamlessly fit into a network management platform.

Stand-Alone Management Applications

Although management platforms provide many benefits, there are circumstances in which they may not be present. These circumstances require the need of a stand-alone management application that can manage a device or a set of devices directly. These circumstances are typically more focused in cases where a few devices from a particular vendor must be managed. You should not have to rely on a management platform to do something this simple. And you may not want to purchase one either. If a network management platform is present, SNMP++ is designed to take advantage of the platform information. On the other hand, if a platform is not present, SNMP++ can operate in a stand-alone manner.

SNMP DATA REPRESENTATION

Data that are to be exchanged between a manager and agent must be represented in a non-machine-specific manner so that machines with differing architectures can communicate. SNMP utilizes the Abstract Syntax Notation One (ASN.1) for this representation. In addition to ASN.1, a standardized encoding scheme is used to encode and decode ASN.1 information. The encoding scheme used is the Basic Encoding Rules (BER) [Steedman].

Protocol Data Units

When an agent picks up an SNMP request message, the message is passed to the SNMP protocol engine where is it decoded and processed. The engine decodes the message to determine its type and the exact information being requested. If the request is authorized, the request is processed and a response is generated to the manager that issued the request. An SNMP message is comprised of various components that make up a request or response. The SNMP message is defined as shown in Figure 2.6.

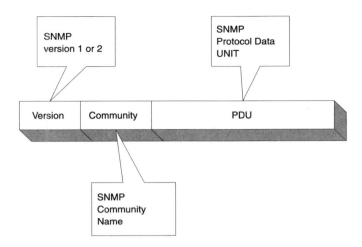

Figure 2.6 SNMP Message.

With the exception of SNMP version 1 trap messages, all SNMP messages have this identical message format. The SNMP version portion of a message defines the version of the SNMP protocol used. There are currently two versions defined, SNMP version 1 and version 2. The *community name* defines a relationship between an agent and a set of managers. The community model applies locally to an agent where every community name defined has a unique view of management information in the MIB. The community names determine a subset of information that may be accessed. This enables different administrative views of an agent's information. For example, a super-manager may want to have full read-write access to all information on an agent, while a monitoring manager might require only read access to a subset of monitoring information. The same community name may have different meanings on different agents. It is, therefore, a manager's responsibility to keep track of which community names apply to which agents.

Encapsulated within an SNMP message is the Protocol Data Unit (PDU). The PDU portion of an SNMP message includes the data to be processed. Every SNMP message includes a PDU. Once the SNMP version number and community name have been verified as correct, the PDU is passed to the protocol engine where it is further decoded. See Figure 2.7 on the next page.

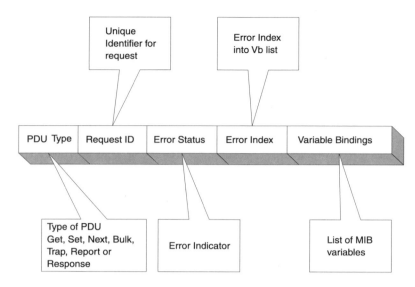

Figure 2.7   SNMP V2 Protocol Data Unit (PDU).

The PDU type determines the type of SNMP transaction or operation in which the PDU is to perform. PDU types are defined in Table 2.2.

Table 2.2   PDU Types.

PDU Type	Description	SNMP version
Get	Utilized for reading MIB information when a manager knows the specific instance information.	SNMP v1 and v2.
Get-Next	Utilized for reading MIB information when a manager does not know the specific instance information.	SNMP v1 and v2.
Response	All SNMP responses utilize the same type.	SNMP v1 and v2.
Set	Utilized for modification of an MIB variable.	SNMP v1 and v2.
Get-Bulk	Utilized for bulk access of MIB variables.	SNMP v2 only.
Inform	Utilized for SNMP inform operation.	SNMP v2 only.
Trap	Unacknowledged SNMP notification PDU.	SNMP v1 and v2.
Report	SNMP report PDU type.	SNMP v2 only.

Each PDU has a unique request identifier that is used to identify the PDU. The request identifier comes in handy when a protocol engine deals with many concurrent PDUs. A well-behaved manager should use a different request identifier for each PDU. Certainly, one cannot always use a different value since they are represented by integers, but back-to-back PDUs should not use the same value. The error status and error index values are use to store error information regarding a PDU. An agent processing a PDU may find that the request is illegal or that it is unable to service the request. Error status determines if an error is present. Error index is used to reference the Variable Binding (Vb) that is in error.

> For SNMP version 1, if a PDU is in error then none of the Variable Bindings (Vbs) are deemed to be valid (error status indicates this error). For SNMP version 2 however, a partially correct PDU may be processed. In this case, the error status value indicates success and individual Vbs hold their own error values represented as Vb exceptions.

The last, and most important, portion of a PDU is the payload or Variable Binding List (VBL). This list includes all of the SNMP variables and their associated values, dependent on the PDU type. Variable bindings are the information that a manager reads, writes, or reports. All SNMP operations require a Variable Binding List to specify precisely the information being accessed or modified.

Variable Bindings

Each SNMP Variable Binding (Vb) consists of a variable and an associated value. Variables are represented by Management Information Base (MIB) object identifiers. Every data item in an MIB can be identified by an object identifier. In addition to the object identifier, each Vb has an associated value. The value can take on one of many SNMP data types. See Figure 2.8 on the next page.

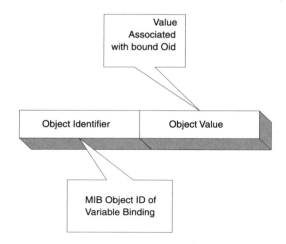

Figure 2.8   Variable Binding.

The Object Identifier (OID) is a unique identifier for referencing an MIB object. The "bound" value represents the value associated with the OID. For Get, Get-Next, and Get-Bulk type PDUs, the value portion is not set or is set to NULL. This is because the value requested is not yet encoded within the PDU. Responses to Get, Get-Next, or Get-Bulk PDUs have valid value portions that represent the requested data.

Object Identifiers

An SNMP object identifier (OID) is a data type that represents a named SNMP object that has been defined in an MIB. OIDs enable the identification of managed objects to be accessed, referenced, or modified. An OID is a sequence of unsigned integers that define a traversal order in an MIB tree. The tree consists of a root and a set of subnodes in which each node in the tree has its own unique identifier and label.

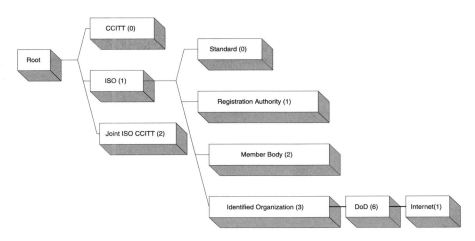

Figure 2.9 MIB Tree.

An OID can be represented in two formats: a dotted integer notation or a friendly name notation. The dotted integer notation uses only unsigned integers separated by dots (periods) to denote a traversal order within an MIB tree. For example, in the tree shown in Figure 2.9, "`1.3.6.1`" represents the `Internet` branch of the tree. Alternatively, the friendly name usage can be used. For friendly name notation, "`iso.org.dod.internet`" represents the same branch of the tree using labels. For machine representation, the dotted unsigned integer notation is used. This is easier to store and compute. For user representation, the friendly name format is easier to read and comprehend.

Structure of Management Information (SMI) Types

In addition to object identifiers, a number of other SNMP data types are required in order to provide useful management information. Since all data types are represented using ASN.1, the data types must be either part of or derived from ASN.1. There are primitive data types, as shown in Table 2.3 on the next page, which allow for the creation of other data types.

Table 2.3   ASN.1 Primitive Types.

ASN.1 Primitive Type Name	Description
INTEGER	An integer value.
OCTET STRING	A data type that can hold zero or more octets. An octet is an 8-bit wide value. Octets can be used to store ASCII strings or binary encoded information.
NULL	A data type that has no value. Null is used to denote a value that contains no value or has yet to be initialized.
OBJECT IDENTIFIER	A data type that holds an object identifier for an MIB object. Object identifiers are stored using "dotted integer representation."
SEQUENCE	A data type that represents an ordered list of zero or more elements. Sequence allows definition of lists of other ASN.1 data types.

In order to provide useful management information, more data types are required. Using the primitive data types, more useful data types may be constructed. The data types are defined with standard MIB definitions. The Structure of Management Information (SMI) defines a set of rules to describe management information using the ASN.1 syntax. This allows management information to be defined independent of a particular implementation. SMI types are defined using ASN.1. The SMI definitions include a set of rules for the designing MIBs including data types for the "SYNTAX" of each MIB object. See Table 2.4.

Table 2.4   SMI Data Types.

SMI Data Types	Description
IpAddress	Representation of an Internet Protocol address.
Counter32	Representation of a non-negative data type used for counting. Internally, this is a 32-bit value. It may increase monotonically until a maximum value is reached, when it will wrap back to a 0 value.

Counter64	Representation of a non-negative data type used for counting. Internally, this is a 64-bit value. It may increase monotonically until a maximum value is reached, when it will wrap back to a 0 value. *(Available in SNMP version 2 only)*
Gauge32	Representation of a non-negative data type used for gauging. Internally, this is a 32-bit value. Its value may increase or decrease. If the value exceeds the maximum value then it latches to the maximum value. If the value later drops below the maximum value then the actual value thereafter can change.
TimeTicks	Representation of a non-negative data type used for the relative time representation. TimeTicks are measured in hundredths of a second relative to some time epoch (typically time since reboot).
Unsigned32	Representation of a data type used when a signed integer will not suffice. Internally, this is a 32-bit value.

These data types enable the complete instrumentation of an agent. SNMP++ has been designed to provide C++ classes for these commonly used data types. For each of these SMI data types, SNMP++ provides a matching C++ class.

PROTOCOL INTERACTIONS

An SNMP manager and agent interact through SNMP protocol transactions. A manager has the ability to read or write information from an agent. Typically a manager requests information from an agent. We therefore have a request/response type of protocol. See Figure 2.10.

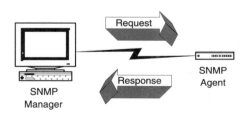

Figure 2.10   SNMP Request / Response.

A request/response protocol requires a manager to poll an agent to determine its state. Although this mechanism works, it can be very inefficient. For managers who manage a large number of devices, it becomes quite burdensome to poll every agent in a management domain. This can be especially true when no fault conditions occur. Furthermore, some network topologies require use of expensive Wide Area Network (WAN) links, making polling cost prohibitive. A more powerful mechanism is to allow the agent to notify the manager when a particular event has occurred. Basically, "We won't call you; you call us instead when there is a problem." In SNMP, this is referred to as event notification. (See Figure 2.11.) In SNMP version 1 notifications are Traps; in SNMP version 2, Informs or Traps can be utilized.

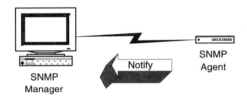

Figure 2.11   SNMP Notifications.

Request/Response Interactions

The SNMP protocol allows four different request/response messages to access and modify management information on an agent. For these kinds of requests, it is the manager's responsibility to formulate the request, send it to the agent, and wait for a response. Since SNMP is designed to operate over connectionless type protocols, a response may not be received. In general, requests and responses may be lost, duplicated, or reordered. In order to compensate for these deficiencies, the manager must decide how to deal with these problems. SNMP++ addresses each of these problems and provides the application developer with transparent reliability. See Table 2.5.

Table 2.5 SNMP Request Types.

SNMP Request Type	Description
Get	Used for reading information when the exact object instance is known. Get requests generate the normal SNMP Response PDU with the requested information.
Get-Next	Used for reading information when the exact instance is not known. The Get-Next request returns the next instance of the one requested in an SNMP Response PDU. A Get-Next request PDU can contain multiple Get-Next variable bindings.
Get-Bulk	Used for reading information in bulk. Get-Bulk improves on the deficiencies of Get-Next when reading tables. *(SNMP version 2 only)*
Set	Used for writing information when the exact object instance is known. Returned is a response PDU with appropriate error status and error index values that indicate the status of the Set.

Notifications

SNMP notifications are used by an agent to notify a manager of an event. The two forms of notifications are the *trap* and the *inform*. (See Table 2.6.) Traps are an unacknowledged SNMP message. That is, no response message is generated. The Inform SNMP message is an acknowledged notification for which the receiver of the Inform message must respond with an SNMP Response message upon acceptance.

Table 2.6 Notification Types.

SNMP Notification Type	Description
Trap	An unacknowledged SNMP message.
Inform	An acknowledged SNMP message generated by an agent or manager. The normal SNMP Response is used as the acknowledgment. *(SNMP version 2 only)*

SNMP VERSION 1

SNMP version 1 can be credited for the success of SNMP. Version 1 was simple to implement, did not use too much computing resources, and provided for an extensible network management framework. In all respects, SNMP version 1 was as simple as possible in order to achieve the requirements of management. SNMP version 1 provided the basic Get, Set, Get-Next, and Trap operations.

When SNMP version 1 was designed, there were a number of features that were not tackled. The idea was to let SNMP version 1 proceed with an easy-to-implement solution and to address newer features later. As SNMP version 1 was deployed, there were a number of areas identified for refinement in version 2. These included an efficient bulk operation for grabbing large amounts of data, new data types for instrumentation of high-speed counters, improved error status codes, and security. Of all these features, security turned out to be the most needed and the most difficult to define.

SNMP VERSION 2

SNMP version 2 addressed many of the deficiencies of version 1. Version 2 enhancements include the "awesome" Get-Bulk operation, 64-bit Counters, improved error codes, and no security. After a great deal of work the IETF SNMP v2 working group was unable to reach an agreement on a standard for SNMP security. The lack of a secure SNMP protocol has prevented SNMP from being used in many environments where security is important. By allowing SNMP version 2 to proceed without much-desired security features, MIBs could be designed using the other desperately needed v2 features. Since MIBs are independent of the protocol used to access them, this makes good sense. See Table 2.7.

Table 2.7   SNMP Version 2 Features.

SNMP Version 2 Feature	Description
Get-Bulk	Enables efficient bulk reading of MIB information.
Counter64	Enables use of 64-bit counters. Good for variables that wrap frequently when Counter32 is used.
Improved Error Codes	Enables individual PDU variable bindings to succeed where others can fail. SNMP version 1 is all or nothing.
New Trap Format	A new trap format makes V2 traps just like any other PDU. This simplifies traps and provides more flexibility.
Inform PDU	The Inform PDU is valuable for manager-to-manager communication, as well as in situations where acknowledged notifications are needed.
Variable Binding Exceptions	V2 enables individual Vbs to be in error while the remaining payload is valid. V1 required that all Vbs in a PDU be correct.

CHAPTER 3

Object-Oriented Programming

This chapter is meant to give an overview of Object-Oriented Programming (OOP), its benefits, usage, and how it can be applied to network and systems management. SNMP++ is more than just an Application Programmers Interface (API). To take full advantage of SNMP++ and achieve reusable, easy-to-maintain code, a good understanding of Object Orientation (OO) is required. Rather than rewrite what has already been said about OO, this chapter focuses on what you need to understand and utilize the OO features of SNMP++. Readers who are already familiar with the OO paradigm and its methodologies may skip this chapter.

OBJECT ORIENTATION

OO programming represents a way of thinking and a methodology for computer programming that are different from the traditional top-down structured programming technique. OO languages provide powerful features that support OO concepts that make computer problem solving more straightforward. An OO approach differs in that the problem space is defined in terms of objects that encapsulate real world objects. These

43

objects encapsulate data and behavior. This alternative view offers many benefits superior to the traditional programming model. A false assumption of traditional programming has been that if OO techniques are used a performance penalty must be paid. It has been shown over and over again that complex systems designed and constructed using an OO approach are easier to develop and maintain, especially where performance is a major concern. Sure, you can implement a program using assembly language and achieve better performance. For that matter, you can also implement it in machine language. An OO approach enables a system to take advantage of the availability of increased hardware capability at a reduced cost.

In its purest sense, OO is achieved by sending messages to objects. With this in mind, a problem solution is devised through the identification of the objects, messages, and object-message sequences that solve a problem. Object-oriented Analysis (OOA) and Design (OOD) employs methodologies for the definition of a problem in OO terms. A problem solution can contain many objects. Some objects that have similar properties can be grouped together. This allows the concept of grouping similar objects into class hierarchies.

PROBLEMS ADDRESSED BY OBJECT ORIENTATION

An OO approach to computer programming allows complex problems to be abstracted into easy-to-understand and easy-to-implement systems. Object modeling allows a system to be modeled in terms of the objects and the relationships between objects in a system. These relationships include static and dynamic behavior. Decomposition of complex systems using a top-down design often yields systems that are difficult to maintain and extend. The true benefit of OO is reuse. This includes reuse of designs, design patterns, and reuse of code. OO languages promote reuse by including OO features, like inheritance, as part of the language. True, many of the principles of OO can be emulated using non-object-oriented languages, but why waste time trying to emulate an OO language when you can use a real one instead. To be considered an OO language, the language must support the concepts detailed in Table 3.1.

Table 3.1   Features of Object Orientation.

Object-Oriented Language Concept	Description
Abstraction	Includes both data abstractions and functional abstractions.
Encapsulation	In OO systems, the unit of encapsulation is the object in which attributes and behavior are encapsulated in a single entity.
Inheritance	The ability of an object to inherit data and/or behavior from a parent class, as defined in a class hierarchy.
Polymorphism	The ability of objects to respond differently to the same message.

Objects and Classes

A core concept in OO is that of *objects* and *classes*. An object is the encapsulation of data and behavior. In traditional programming we design programs using data structures and procedures that operate on them. In the OO world, the data and procedures are wrapped into a single element called an object. Programming is accomplished by sending messages to these objects. Classes are definitions of objects.

Abstraction

In the OO sense, abstraction can apply both to data and to functions. Data abstractions are represented by a select class of objects. These are commonly known as Abstract Data Types (ADTs) or *abstract classes*. Those classes which do not embody abstractions are considered *concrete classes*. An example is a class that represents a *network device*. (See Figure 3.1 on the next page.) Subclasses of network device would include *network hub* and *network switch*. The network device class is considered an abstract class because it does not refer to an actual instance of a network device but rather to the concept of an abstract one. The classes hub and switch, on the other hand, refer to concrete classes because they represent actual classes. The ability to define and utilize abstract classes allows the development of code that operates only to abstract objects.

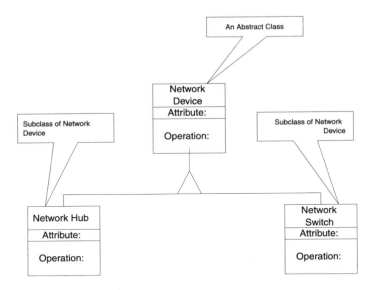

Figure 3.1 Network Device Class.

A different form of abstraction is that of *functional abstraction*. Functional abstraction is achieved by message passing. For example, consider the abstract message *reset* that would apply to the preceding abstract network device object.

Encapsulation

Encapsulation enables the concept of data hiding in which the attributes and behavior can be contained within an object. Encapsulation is achieved in traditional programming languages through the use of the "struct" or structure. In the OO sense, encapsulation is extended to include not only data but behavior as well. This enables the clean definition of an object for which the interface is clearly defined and exposed. Additionally, OO encapsulation enables the definition of protection of attributes and behavior. That is, attributes and behavior can be defined as *public, private,* or *protected.* Public interfaces are those that are exposed to the outside world or users of the object. All non-public attributes and behavior are internal to the object itself and therefore are of no interest to the outside user of the object. This provides what is known as data hiding.

A properly designed object exposes message interfaces for all interaction. This is in contrast to exposing data attributes directly.

Inheritance

The concept of class hierarchy, in which some classes are subordinate to others, facilitates inheritance. Subclasses are considered to be specialized cases of the class under which they are grouped in the hierarchy. The lower levels of the hierarchy represent increased specialization, while the upper levels represent more generalization. This allows a class hierarchy to be developed in which the uppermost class can be considered an abstract class that embodies the attributes and behavior of all the subclasses. Well, almost. Subclasses, as they are more specialized, may wish to introduce or redefine new attributes or behavior. By default, all attributes and behavior of a parent class are defined to be inherited. If a parent class embodies certain characteristics, these are inherited by the subclasses. The major benefit this enables is extensibility for which the addition of a new class entails only adding or redefining characteristics, everything else being inherited.

Polymorphism

Polymorphism enables an identical message to be sent to different objects with each object responding to that message in a manner appropriate to the type of object it is. For example, say we have a class hierarchy representing a network address. The hierarchy is shown in Figure 3.2 on the next page.

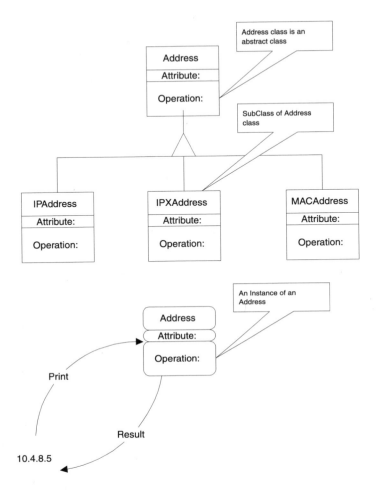

Figure 3.2   Polymorphism.

Given an Address object, we can send it a message to print itself out. We can send this message to any Address object. The returned result, however, will differ based on the actual Address subclass that exists. For the preceding example, the actual Address object is an IPAddress. We therefore get a dotted IP address string when we send it the *print* message. By using abstract objects and polymorphism, interfaces to objects can be reused.

WHY OBJECT ORIENTATION WORKS

Rather than simply accept OO technology hook, line, and sinker, it is important to appreciate why OO works. OO technology has been adopted in almost all areas of software development. This is due to more than just hype. Think what it would be like to develop systems where no OO technology could be used: we would have to resort to older structured programming techniques. Possessing a methodology and language that promote good design and implementation, everything is easier, and the result is the ability to focus on the problem you are trying to solve, not the technique you use to solve it. Object-oriented programming (OOP) is the programming methodology of choice. It is the product of over 25 years of programming and system design experience. For systems that are complex, such as network management systems, OO offers many attractive benefits.

OBJECT-ORIENTED ANALYSIS AND DESIGN

There is more to OO than merely an implementation. In addition, a methodology is required that allows for the analysis and design of OO systems. Analysis deals with *what* components make up a system. This is in contrast to design, where one is concerned with *how* the system is implemented. In an OO context, analysis is concerned with the definition of *what* objects and methods make up a system solution. OO analysis defines the identification of objects that model the system and the relationship between the objects. When designing OO systems, two views of a system should be considered. This includes a static view of the objects and methods, and a dynamic view that describes the sequence of object-method transactions that devise a solution.

Object Modeling Technique (OMT)

This book utilizes the Object Modeling Technique (OMT), [Rumbaugh] developed by James Rumbaugh for the presentation of OO concepts and SNMP++ designs. OMT supports three different models, including the *Object Model, Dynamic Model,* and *Functional Model.* Some basic OMT symbols utilized in this text are defined in the sections that follow.

OMT Class   The symbol for a class includes the name of the class, its attributes, and operations. The class symbol is represented by a squared-corner rectangle. Once a class is defined, it can be referenced only by its name. Because the class is only a definition, it does not represent a live instance of an object. See Figure 3.3.

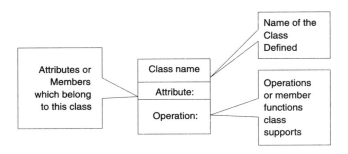

Figure 3.3   OMT Class Symbol.

OMT Object (Instance of a Class)   An object is an instance of a class. In OMT, it is represented by a rounded-corner rectangle. The name of an object reflects the class name of which it is an instance. See Figure 3.4.

Figure 3.4   OMT Object Symbol.

OMT Generalization (Inheritance)   Generalization is a type of association between two or more classes. The OMT symbol denoting generalization is a line with an arrow. (See Figure 3.5.) The arrow points up to the class that the association is to be generalized from. Generalization allows the definition of inheritance. This is also known as the "is-a" relationship. For example, *ATM Switch* "is-a" *Switch*. Using the generalization symbols, class hierarchies can be designed.

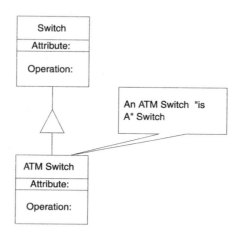

Figure 3.5 OMT Generalization Symbol.

OMT Association Another important type of association is the "has-a" association. The OMT symbol denoting this relationship is simply a line connecting two classes. (See Figure 3.6.) This type of relationship describes loose association. For example, consider a *network hub*. A *network hub* "has-a" *power supply*. The *power supply* is itself an object.

Network Hub		Power Supply
Attribute:		Attribute:
Operation:		Operation:

Figure 3.6 OMT "Has-A" Association Symbol.

OMT Aggregation   Another type of association that denotes containment is the aggregation symbol. (See Figure 3.7.) This is also known as the "consists-of" relationship. For example, consider a network hub that has ports (interfaces). We can model this as a hub that "consists-of" ports. The port is an object as well.

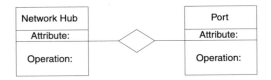

Figure 3.7   OMT Aggregation Symbol.

OMT Object Model

The OMT Object Model allows for the definition of a static model of the system on which its components are organized into workable components. This model describes real-world classes and their relationships to one another and to the outside world. The two most important relationships modeled in the object model are *generalizations* and *associations*. Generalizations show inheritance or *is-a* relationships, while associations show containment or *has-a* relationships. Together, the ability to represent classes and their relationships graphically make the Object Model a powerful tool for designing object-oriented systems. This book utilizes the OMT Object Model for all SNMP++ class definitions.

OMT Dynamic Model

The OMT Dynamic Model shows the time-dependent behavior of objects within a system. Using the Dynamic Model, the object-message interactions can be modeled in the sequence in which they occur. This model is important for dynamic systems such as real-time systems.

OMT Functional Model

The OMT Functional Model shows a functional partitioning of a system. This allows a functional decomposition of a system based on objects. The Functional Model utilizes the objects and flows of data between objects to show functional dependencies. This allows clear definition of the input and output of a system.

C++

C++ was developed by Bjarne Stroustrup in the early 1980s at AT&T Bell Labs [Stroustrup]. Stroustrup had two main goals in mind when creating C++. First of all, C++ had to be compatible with ordinary C, and second, C had to be extended with object-oriented constructs. An ultimate goal of C++ is to provide a language the professional programmer can use to develop object-oriented software without a sacrificing C's efficiency or portability. In addition to supporting the object-oriented paradigm, C++ offers many benefits.

A Better C

Since C++ is based mostly on C, it retains much of C's language, including a rich operator set, extensibility, and the ability to write terse code. Like C, C++ is highly portable. Unlike other object-oriented languages such as Smalltalk, C++ is quite inexpensive. You don't need a *Graphical User Interface* (GUI) environment or significant increase in memory or computing resources. C++ improves C by its support of strong typing. This makes C++ a safer language to use. A programmer using C++ can easily reuse code that was constructed using C. This allows reuse of code that was previously developed and prevents the rewrite of code just for the sake of going to a new language. C++ can be thought of as a superset of C.

Data Abstraction and Encapsulation

Data abstraction and encapsulation are provided in C++ through the use of the *class* construct. Like the C *struct*, the C++ *class* allows the representation of *Abstract Data Types* (ADTs). Unlike the C *struct*, the

C++ *class* allows the specification of *private* and *protected* members. Thus the ADT concept is strengthened. In addition, the C++ *class* allows inheritance and polymorphism through subclassing and virtual member functions.

Operator Overloading

C++ allows overloading operators. This enables C++ to provide an extremely natural syntax for new data types or classes that are introduced. SNMP++ utilizes overloaded operators in a variety of places to provide a safe and natural syntax for dealing with SNMP data types. Compared to an SNMP API constructed using only C, SNMP++ is cleaner, safer, and more powerful.

C H A P T E R 4

Introduction to SNMP++

Various Simple Network Management
Protocol (SNMP) Application Programmers Interfaces (APIs) exist that
make the creation of network management applications possible. The
majority of these APIs provide a large library of functions that require
programmers to be familiar with the inner workings of SNMP and with
SNMP resource management. Most of these APIs are platform-specific,
resulting in SNMP code specific to an operating system or to a network
operating system platform and thus not portable. Application development using C++ has entered the mainstream, and with its coming a rich
set of reusable class libraries is now readily available. What is missing is
a standard set of C++ classes for network management. An object-oriented approach to SNMP network programming provides many benefits,
including ease-of-use, safety, portability, and extensibility. SNMP++
offers power and flexibility that would otherwise be difficult to implement and manage.

SNMP++ is a set of C++ classes that provides SNMP services to a
network management application developer. SNMP++ brings the object
advantage to network management programming. SNMP++ represents
the coming together of two technologies: network management and object
orientation. Bringing these two technologies together yields many benefits.

55

HISTORY OF SNMP++

SNMP++ was conceived in the fall of 1994. At that time there were a number of compelling reasons to provide an object-oriented approach to network management development. Because engineers on network management teams were confronting a variety of problems, including reliability, robustness, extensibility, and cross-platform support of SNMP code, the idea of SNMP++ evolved. At the time SNMP++ was conceived, there were no tools for the development of SNMP applications across multiple platforms. Furthermore, there were no OO or C++ based libraries available. Teams at Hewlett-Packard and within the industry as a whole were looking for a solution to the problem. Such teams were staffing experts to solve the problems but with much replication and waste. For example, in the area of cross-platform support, experts were required for each platform. So, the MS-Windows team had one set of tools, the HP-UNIX team had a different set of tools, and the Sun Solaris team had their own set of tools. This strategy worked but was expensive and hard to manage since such a large number of experts was required. Rather than one or two SNMP experts, each team would have four or five. Not only was the development effort wasted, so was the testing effort. Worst of all, if someone wanted to fix something or add features, it had to be done across all platforms. This made extensibility an enormous challenge.

Clearly, one common set of code that could operate across all target operating systems would be of great value. Prior to SNMP++, SNMP APIs were not object-oriented. Most application developers in the 1990s use an object-oriented approach toward code development. This includes OO analysis, OO design, and most significantly, OO implementation. It seemed crazy that developers used powerful development tools such as Microsoft Visual C++ for their applications, but when it came to SNMP-related code they used a 1970s-style Kernigan and Ritchie C approach [K&R]. Considering that the real muscle behind a network management application is contained in the SNMP code, a OO SNMP API was sorely needed.

WinSNMP++

In 1994, a new SNMP API hit the street. This API was an SNMP API for Microsoft Windows (MS-Windows), WinSNMP [WinSNMP]. The MS-Windows environment has many special architectural features, so a MS-Windows-specific SNMP API was required. The model for WinSNMP was much like Windows Sockets (WinSockets) [WinSock]. Both WinSock and WinSNMP were initially presented at the Networld + Interop conference with success that turned them into industry, or de facto, standards. With the introduction of WinSNMP, the definition for another API, WinSNMP++, was briefly specified. Basically, this API added C++ extensions to all WinSNMP functions. Unfortunately since this was focused primarily on MS-Windows, it did not allow for clean portability to other operating systems. The specification for WinSNMP++ did, however, strengthen the idea of SNMP++. An implementation of WinSNMP++ was never achieved.

Hewlett-Packard SNMP++

In early 1994, the Hewlett-Packard Company (HP) embarked on a series of network management projects that required multiple-platform support. Rather than support multiple SNMP APIs, one for each platform, an engineering decision was made to support multiple platforms but to do so using only the SNMP++ API. This eliminated the need for redundant engineers and created the opportunity to design and build a new object-oriented SNMP API. From the beginning, the intent was to make SNMP++ an open specification.

SNMP++ Open Specification

Since the IETF group does not deal with the specification of APIs, it is inappropriate to pursue SNMP++ in the form of an RFC. After much discussion regarding SNMP++ in the WinSNMP mailing group, the decision was made to use the same mailing list for discussion of SNMP++. The initial specification for SNMP++, revision 1.0, was posted to the WinSNMP e-mail group where it was evaluated by many. By spring 1995, an implementation was fully developed by HP. The specification

and experience was described at the Networld + Interop Conference in
the format of Birds-of-a-Feather (BOF) meetings. The specification and
full implementation are freely available at the following World Wide Web
site: *http://rosegarden.external.hp.com/snmp++*.

MOTIVATION

The motivation for the development of SNMP++ stemmed from immediate development problems confronted by engineers at HP. In addition to
immediate needs, such as cross-platform development, there were a variety of other reasons behind the creation of SNMP++.

Too Many APIs

SNMP programming has too many APIs. For the most part they all
do the same thing. There are a number of APIs for SNMP freely available. All of them support a different set of interfaces. Also, there is a
variety of commercial implementations; they, too, have a different set of
interfaces. SNMP++ is designed so that it can and has been implemented
across different platforms using the same API. This enables developers
who need to support multiple platforms to deal with only one API.

Lack of Object Orientation

An OO SNMP API was sorely needed. All of the applications being
developed were utilizing OO tools, including the use of C++. When it
came to SNMP programming, however, we were forced to step back into
the Stone Age and use a cumbersome C API. Since the critical code
underlying any network management application is the SNMP code, it
was determined that the most bang-for-buck could be realized through
the use of an OO SNMP API.

Lack of Simplicity

Many of the existing SNMP APIs were hard to use. This was
because the APIs were C-based and did not allow automatic memory
management through C++ constructors and destructors. Since SNMP
code is the core behind a network management application, any new API

had to be as simple to use as possible. The philosophy was to let the library perform the work. Simplicity must be achieved without sacrificing flexibility. Network management applications are built in many different architectures, and an overly simplified API may preclude many designs. Oversimplification, therefore, should not sacrifice flexibility.

Too Expensive to Develop Multiplatform Applications

Rather than be overly immersed in the technology, the economics of network management development has to be considered. How can network management applications be developed that reach as many platforms as possible at minimum cost? Basically, this boils down to the ability to leverage technology that has already been developed and enable developers to stay focused on the problem they are trying to solve. A network management developer should not have to be concerned with the low-level mechanics of SNMP. A minimal understanding of SNMP is all that is required.

There Has to Be a Better Way!

In many respects, the multitude of SNMP APIs seemed to follow the path of least resistance as they evolved. The result was that these APIs supported a cornucopia of interfaces that seemed unrelated. In short, the overall model of how an application should interface with an SNMP library was unclear. No cross-platform support, no object orientation, difficult to use, no overall model. There has to be a better way!

OBJECTIVES OF SNMP++

Ease of Use and SNMP++

An object-oriented (OO) approach to SNMP programming should be easy to use. After all, this is supposed to be a simple network management protocol. SNMP++ attempts to put the simple back into SNMP. The application programmer does not need to be concerned with low-level SNMP mechanisms. An OO approach to SNMP encapsulates and hides the internal mechanisms of SNMP. In regard to ease of use, SNMP++ addresses the following areas.

Provides an easy-to-use interface to SNMP   A user does not have to be an SNMP expert to use SNMP++. Furthermore, a user does not have to be an expert in C++! For the most part, C pointers do not exist in SNMP++. The result is an easy-to-use straightforward API.

Provides easy migration to SNMP version 2   A major goal of SNMP++ is to develop an Application Programmers Interface (API) that scales to SNMP version 2 with minimal impact on code. The SNMP++ SnmpTarget class makes this possible.

Preserves the flexibility of lower-level SNMP programming   A user may want to bypass the OO approach and code directly to low-level SNMP calls. SNMP++ is fast and efficient, but there may be instances where the programmer requires coding directly to a lower-level SNMP API.

Encourages programmers to use the full power of C++ without chastising them for not learning fast enough   A user does not have to be an expert in C++ to use SNMP++. Basic knowledge of SNMP is required, but only a minimal understanding of C++ is needed. More advanced users of C++ may wish to subclass their own vendor-specific classes from the basic SNMP++ classes.

Programming Safety and SNMP++

Most SNMP APIs require the programmer to manage a variety of resources. Improper allocation or de-allocation of these resources can result in corrupted or lost memory. SNMP++ provides safety by managing these resources automatically. The user of SNMP++ realizes the benefits of automatic resource and session management. In regard to programming safety, SNMP++ addresses the following areas.

Provides safe management of SNMP resources   This includes SNMP structures, sessions, and transport layer management. SNMP classes are designed as Abstract Data Types (ADTs) to provide data hiding and provide public member functions to inspect or modify hidden instance variables.

Provides built-in error checking, automatic time-out, and retry A user of SNMP++ does not have to be concerned with providing reliability for an unreliable transport mechanism. A variety of communications errors can occur, including lost datagrams, duplicated datagrams, and reordered datagrams. SNMP++ addresses each of these possible error conditions and provides the user with transparent reliability.

Portability and SNMP++

A major goal of SNMP++ is to provide an API that is portable across a variety of operating systems (OSs), network operating systems (NOSs), and network management platforms. Since the internal mechanisms of SNMP++ are hidden, the public interface remains the same across any platform. A programmer who codes to SNMP++ does not have to make any changes to move it to another platform. Another issue in the area of portability is the ability to run across a variety of protocols. SNMP++ currently operates over the Internet Protocol (IP), or Internet Packet Exchange (IPX) protocols, or both, using a dual stack. See Figure 4.1.

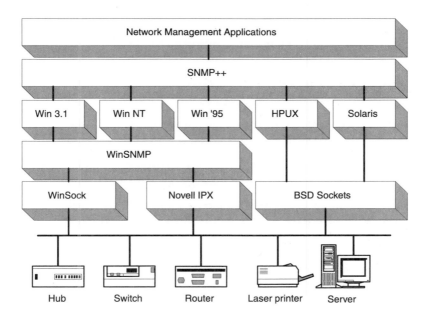

Figure 4.1 SNMP++ Portability.

Extensibility and SNMP++

Extensibility is not a binary function but rather one of degree. SNMP++ can be extended easily. Extensions to SNMP++ include support of new OSs, NOSs, network management platforms, protocols, support of SNMP version 2, and the addition of new features. Through C++ class derivation, users of SNMP++ can inherit what they like and overload what they wish to redefine.

Overloading SNMP++ Base Classes   The application programmer can subclass the base SNMP++ classes to produce specialized behavior and attributes. This theme is central to object orientation. The base classes of SNMP++ are meant to be generic and do not contain any vendor-specific data structures or behavior. New attributes can be added easily through C++ subclassing and virtual member function redefinition.

SNMP++ FEATURES

Full Set of C++ Based SNMP Classes

SNMP++ is based upon a set of C++ classes, including the Object Identifier (Oid) class, Variable Binding (Vb) class, Protocol Data Unit (Pdu) class, Snmp class, and a variety of other classes, making work with Abstract Syntax Notation (ASN.1) Structure of Management Information (SMI) types easy and object-oriented.

Automatic SNMP Memory Management

The classes manage various SNMP structures and resources automatically when objects are instantiated and destroyed. This frees the application programmer worrying about de-allocating structures and resources and thus provides better protection from memory corruption and leaks. SNMP++ objects can be instantiated statically or dynamically. Static object instantiation allows destruction when the object goes out of scope. Dynamic allocation requires use of C++ constructs *new* and *delete*. Internal to SNMP++ are various Structure of Management Information (SMI) structures that are protected and hidden from the public interface. All SMI structures are managed internally: the programmer does not need to define or manage SMI structures or values. For the most part, usage of "C" pointers in SNMP++ is nonexistent.

Ease of Use

SNMP++ classes are easy and safe to use because all SMI structures are hidden and managed. The programmer cannot corrupt what is hidden and protected from his or her scope of action.

Power and Flexibility

SNMP++ provides power and flexibility that would otherwise be difficult to implement and manage. Each SNMP++ object communicates with an agent through a session model. That is, an instance of an SNMP++ session class maintains connections to specified agents. Each SNMP++ object provides reliability through automatic retry and timeouts. An application may have multiple SNMP++ object instances, each instance communicating to the same or different agent(s). This is a powerful feature that enables a network management application to have different sessions for each management component. Alternatively, a single Snmp session can be used for everything. For example, an application may have one SNMP++ Snmp object to provide graphing statistics, another SNMP++ Snmp object to monitor traps, and a third SNMP++ Snmp object to enable SNMP browsing. SNMP++ automatically handles multiple concurrent requests from different SNMP++ instances.

Portable Objects

The majority of SNMP++ is portable C++ code. Only the Snmp class implementation is different for each target operating system. If your program contains SNMP++ code, this code will port without any changes!

Automatic Time-Out and Retries

SNMP++ supports automatic time-out and retries. This frees the programmer from having to implement time-out or retry code. Retransmission policy is defined in the SnmpTarget class. This allows each managed target to have its own time-out/retry policy.

Blocked Mode Requests

SNMP++ includes a blocked model. The blocked mode for MS-Windows allows multiple blocked requests on separate SNMP class instances.

Non-Blocking Asynchronous Mode Requests

SNMP++ also supports a non-blocking asynchronous mode for requests. Time-outs and retries are supported in both blocked and asynchronous modes.

Notifications, Trap Reception, and Sending

SNMP++ is designed to allow trap reception and sending of multiple transports, including IP and IPX. In addition, SNMP++ allows trap reception and sending using non-standard trap IP ports and IPX socket numbers.

Support for SNMP Versions 1 and 2 Through a Bilingual API

SNMP++ has been designed with support and usage for SNMP versions 1 and 2. All operations within the API are designed to be bilingual. That is, operations are not SNMP-specific. Through utilization of the SnmpTarget class, SNMP version-specific operations are abstracted.

SNMP Get, Get-Next, Get-Bulk, Set, Inform, and Trap Supported

SNMP++ supports all six SNMP operations. All six SNMP++ member functions utilize similar parameter lists and operate in a blocked or non-blocked (asynchronous) manner.

Redefinition Through Inheritance

SNMP++ is implemented using C++ and thus enables programmers to overload or redefine behavior that does not meet their needs. For example, if an application has special Oid object needs, a subclass of the Oid class can be created, inheriting all the attributes and behavior of the Oid base class while allowing new behavior and attributes to be added to the derived class.

A SIMPLE SNMP++ EXAMPLE

Rather than begin with a description of SNMP++ and all of its features, Example 4.1 illustrates the power and simplicity of SNMP++. This example obtains an SNMP MIB System Descriptor object from the specified agent. Included is all the code you need to create an SNMP++ session, get the system descriptor, and print it out.

Retries and time-outs are managed automatically. The SNMP++ code is in bold font.

Example 4.1   A Simple SNMP++ Example.

```cpp
#define SYSDESCR "1.3.6.1.2.1.1.1.0"        // Object ID for System Descriptor
void get_system_descriptor()
{
    int status;                             // return status
    CTarget ctarget( (IpAddress) "10.4.8.5");// SNMP++ community target
    Vb vb( SYSDESCR);                       // SNMP++ Variable Binding Object
    Pdu pdu;                                // SNMP++ PDU

    //----[ Construct an SNMP++ SNMP Object ]------------------
    Snmp snmp( status);                     // Create an SNMP++ session
    if ( status != SNMP_CLASS_SUCCESS) {    // check creation status
        cout << snmp.error_msg( status);    // if fail, print error string
        return;   }

    //----[ Invoke an SNMP++ Get ]--------------------
    pdu += vb;                              // append the vb to the PDU
    if (  (status = snmp.get( pdu, ctarget)) != SNMP_CLASS_SUCCESS)
        cout << snmp.error_msg( status);
    else {
        pdu.get_vb( vb,0);                  // extract the vb from PDU
        cout << "System Descriptor = "<< vb.get_printable_value();
    }                                       // print out the value

};                                          // Thats all!
```

Output
```
System Descriptor = MS-Windows NT 4.0
```

Explanation of Introductory Example

The actual SNMP++ calls are made up of ten lines of code. A Community Based Target (CTarget) object is created by acquiring the SNMP object using the IP address of the agent. The default community name of *public* is assumed since one is not specified. A variable binding (Vb) object is then created using the object identifier of the MIB object to retrieve (System Descriptor). The Vb object is then attached to a Pdu object. An Snmp object is used to invoke the SNMP Get transaction. The Get Member function takes a Pdu and a Target object. The Pdu holds the data to be retrieved and the CTarget describes where the data is to be retrieved from. Once retrieved, the response message is printed out. All error-handling code is included.

Part II:
The SNMP++ Framework

CHAPTER 5

The Operational Model

This chapter focuses on the SNMP++ operational model and the classes that make up the SNMP++ framework. The classes that make up SNMP++ and the relationships that exist between them are examined in depth.

THE SNMP++ FRAMEWORK

A framework is a set of classes that cooperate to make up a reusable design for a specific class of software. SNMP++ consists of such a set of classes that enable the reuse of the classes as a whole. This framework dictates the architecture of your application. In doing so, a framework is a type of design pattern, or reusable design [Gamma]. A framework helps to define the overall design by partitioning classes and objects and their interaction. Frameworks are increasingly common and important. Simply by developing a set of classes that model a problem domain is not sufficient. An API design also should include the interaction of the classes and objects that are necessary to write useful applications. The SNMP++ framework predefines design parameters in which an application can be developed. SNMP++ has evolved through field use and implementation experience. In the beginning, SNMP++ was just a set of atomic classes that were used as separate pieces. Soon it was realized that the true value of an OO SNMP API was in providing a complete set of classes that function together collectively.

The OMT model that follows in Figure 5.1 shows the various SNMP++ classes and the relationships among them.

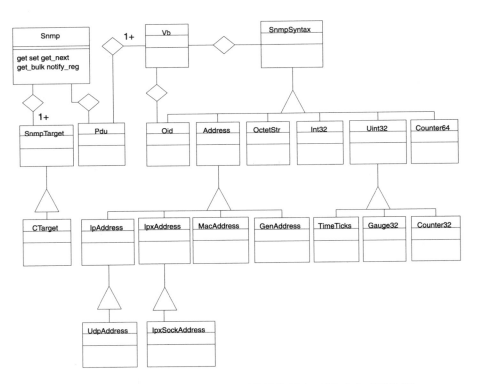

Figure 5.1   Object Modeling Technique (OMT) Object Model of SNMP++
Framework.

SNMP SYNTAX CLASSES

The basic elements of SNMP are the Structure of Management (SMI) Abstract Syntax Notation One (ASN.1) Syntax data elements. A Management Information Base (MIB) is comprised of these values. An MIB is represented by various SMI values that can be accessed or modified by a manager application. The SNMP++ SNMP Syntax classes represent an object-oriented C++ view of SMI data types that are used by SNMP. Included is a set of classes that map to their equivalent SMI types. In addition, a few non-SMI classes have been introduced for usefulness and power. SNMP++ gives these SNMP data types a powerful, easy-to-use interface. A brief description of the various SNMP++ syntax classes follows and is shown in Figure 5.2.

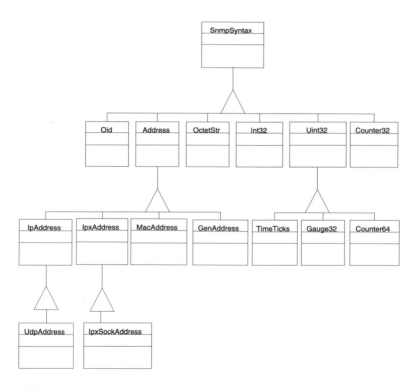

Figure 5.2   Object Modeling Technique (OMT) Object Model of SNMP++ Syntax Classes.

The base class of the Syntax classes is the SnmpSyntax class. This is an abstract class. No instances of this class are allowed. The benefit of this abstract class is that a variety of virtual member functions can be appreciated by all derived classes of SnmpSyntax. In addition, C++ operator overloading is utilized to make working with SNMP values as easy as working with simple integers. The basic class hierarchy includes classes for object identifiers, network addresses, octet strings, integers, counters, and gauges. The network address class and unsigned integer class have derived classes of their own in order to support more specific attributes and behavior. It is important to state that the SnmpSyntax class hierarchy can be extended to meet a particular application's needs through custom class derivation. SnmpSyntax classes also support full automatic memory management so that when any SnmpSyntax object is constructed or modified, it allocates all the resources it requires auto- matically. Conversely, the destructors automatically free up all resources. Automatic memory management reduces memory leaks and eases development.

Table 5.1 shows the various SnmpSyntax classes and how they map to existing SNMP Structure of Management Information (SMI) or Abstract Syntax Notation One (ASN.1) values.

Table 5.1   SNMP++ Classes and Related Structure of Management Information Data Types.

SNMP++ Syntax Class Name	Class Description	SMI or ASN.1 Counterpart
SnmpSyntax	Parent of all syntax classes.	No ASN.1 counterpart, used for OO structure.
Oid	Object identifier class.	ASN.1 Object Identifier.
OctectStr	Octet string class.	ASN.1 Octet string.
Uint32	Unsigned 32-bit integer class.	SMI unsigned 32-bit integer.
TimeTicks	TimeTicks class.	SMI time ticks.
Counter32	32-bit counter class.	SMI 32-bit counter.
Gauge32	32-bit gauge class.	SMI 32-bit gauge.
Int32	Signed 32-bit integer.	SMI 32-bit signed integer.

Counter64	64-bit counter class.	SMI 64-bit counter.
Address	Abstract address class.	No ASN.1 counterpart used for OO structure.
IpAddress	IP address class.	SMI IP address.
UdpAddress	UdpAddress class	SMI IP address with port specification.
IpxAddress	IPX address class.	No ASN.1 or SMI counterpart.
IpxSockAddress	IPX Address class with socket number.	No ASN.1 or SMI counterpart.
MacAddress	MAC address class.	SMI counterpart.
GenAddress	Generic Address	No ASN.1 or SMI counterpart.

SNMP++ provides a variety of classes matching the SMI types. These include the Oid class, the OctetStr class, the Counter32 and Counter64 classes, the Gauge32 class, and the TimeTicks class. In addition to these data types, a Management Information Base (MIB) can be made up of plain old integers. SMI supports two types of integers, signed and unsigned 32-bit integers. SNMP++ has two C++ classes that are used in the hierarchy of the SnmpSyntax classes for integers and unsigned integers. They are the Int32 class and the Uint32 class. It should be mentioned that these classes provide the appropriate object model for SNMP++ and don't have to be used in your code when you want to deal with signed and unsigned 32-bit integers. You can use the normal C data types if you like. SNMP++ does, however, provide a proper class hierarchy of the SMI data types.

THE SESSION MODEL

The session is an important concept in SNMP++. A session represents a logical relationship between a manager and agents in which a manager is interacting with one or more agents for every given session. This interaction occurs through SNMP transactions such as Get, Set, Get-Next, or Get-Bulk. A session in SNMP++ is also an object, the Snmp object. A session has a number of important attributes that for the most part are hidden from the public interface. This includes all network interaction with the agent. The Snmp class hides the lower-level Internet Protocol/User

Datagram Protocol (IP/UDP) or Internet Exchange Protocol (IPX) details and complexities and in doing makes interaction with an agent easy. An application can have as many sessions as is required in order to meet a particular design. Sessions have many advantages, including providing a clean encapsulation of the manager-to-agent interaction and enabling automatic transport control.

WORKING WITH SNMP TARGETS

Along with the concept of the SNMP session is the concept of a managed target in which a target represents a managed entity. A managed entity can be an agent or a dual role entity that responds to SNMP requests. A managed entity is more than just a network address. In order to communicate with an SNMP agent effectively, additional information is required. In addition to a network address, the type of protocol, retransmission policy, and community names are required to provide a complete picture of what a manager is managing and how the management is to be accomplished. All SNMP++ transactions require a target. Targets are represented in SNMP++ through the SnmpTarget class hierarchy. See Figure 5.3.

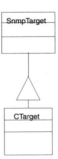

Figure 5.3   Object Modeling Technique (OMT) Object Model View of SnmpTarget Class.

SNMP Community-Based Targets

SNMP version 2 is commonly referred to as "community-based" SNMP version 2. The ASN.1 representations of SNMP version 1 and version 2 messages are nearly identical. This allows the representation of a version 1 or version 2 target using the same class. For SNMP version 1 and version 2, community names are used to define an administrative view of the agent's Management Information Base (MIB). That is, a community name is used to denote a subset of managed information within an agent. Community-based targets are represented using SNMP++ CTarget class. The CTarget class allows definition of the read and write community names, in addition to everything they inherit from the parent SnmpTarget class.

ASYNCHRONOUS AND BLOCKING MODES OF OPERATION

There are two basic modes of operation in SNMP++, blocking and asynchronous. This relates to how response data is delivered back to a management application. Blocking transactions do not return control until they are complete. For example, if a blocked SNMP Get is invoked, it will not return until either the response arrives or an error occurs. Asynchronous calls, on the other hand, return control as soon as the request is issued. The response in asynchronous mode is called back to a caller's provided callback function. Each of these modes have a time and place in a user's application. Blocked mode is great for performing quick transactions that do not occur frequently. Asynchronous mode may be a little more difficult to code, but it integrates well with event systems like those found within MS-Windows. Asynchronous mode lends itself well to periodic activities like polling.

The SnmpSyntax Classes

This chapter defines the various classes within SNMP++ that comprise the SnmpSyntax classes. The SnmpSyntax classes represent the various Abstract Syntax Notation One (ASN.1) and Structure of Management Information (SMI) data types used within SNMP. They are what make up all the *managed objects* of which Management Information Bases (MIBs) are made. Although these data types are called managed objects in the Internet Engineering Task Force (IETF) SNMP standards, in reality they are not object-oriented. When these data types are placed within a C++ class hierarchy, a complete set of object-oriented SNMP C++ classes is available.

THE OBJECT IDENTIFIER CLASS

The Object Identification (Oid) class is the encapsulation of an SMI object identifier. The SMI object identifier is a data identifier for an SNMP object found within a Management Information Base (MIB), as defined by an MIB definition. The SMI Oid and its related structures and functions are a natural fit for object orientation. In fact, the Oid class shares many common features with the C++ String class. For those of you familiar with the C++ String class or Microsoft's Foundation Classes (MFC) CString class, the Oid class will be familiar and easy to use. The

Oid class is designed to be efficient and fast. It allows definition and manipulation of object identifiers. The Oid class may be compiled and used with any ANSI C++ compiler. Of all the data types in SNMP, the object identifier is one of the most used. A full-featured Oid class therefore comes in handy. See Figure 6.1.

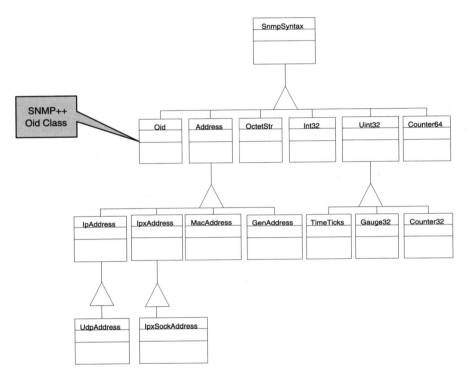

Figure 6.1   Object Modeling Technique (OMT) Object Model View of the SNMP++ Oid Class.

> ❗ The ASN.1 OBJECT IDENTIFIER type represents a sequence of non-negative integers that allow the specification of a *managed object* within an MIB. The sequence of numbers defines a traversal order within a tree. In SNMP, a maximum of 128 sub-ids are allowed for each object identifier.

An Oid object can be constructed in a variety of ways, including construction of an Oid with no information, with a dotted string, with another Oid, or with a pointer and some data. The C++ destructor for the Oid object takes care of all memory and resource de-allocation, making the Oid class easy and safe to use. See Table 6.1.

Table 6.1   Oid Class Constructors and Destructor.

Oid Class Constructors and Destructor	Description
Constructors	
`Oid::Oid( void);`	Construct an empty Oid.
`Oid::Oid( const char *dotted_string);`	Construct an Oid with a dotted string.
`Oid::Oid( const Oid &oid);`	Construct an Oid with another Oid, copy constructor.
`Oid::Oid( const unsigned long *data, int len);`	Construct an Oid with a pointer and length.
Destructor	
`Oid::~Oid( );`	Destroy the Oid, free up all memory held.

A number of member functions are provided to make using the Oid class useful. Of the member functions available, overloaded operators provide a natural look and feel when you work with Oids. See Table 6.2.

Table 6.2   Oid Class Overloaded Operators.

Oid Class Member Functions	Description
Overloaded Operators	
`Oid & operator = ( const char *dotted_string);`	Assign an Oid a dotted string.
`Oid & operator = ( const Oid &oid);`	Assign an Oid an Oid.
`int operator == ( const Oid &lhs, const Oid& rhs);`	Compare two Oids for equivalence.

(continued)

Table 6.2 *(continued)*

Oid Class Member Functions	Description
`int operator == ( const Oid& lhs, const char*dotted_string);`	Compare an Oid & string for equivalence.
`int operator != ( const Oid &lhs, const Oid& rhs);`	Compare two Oids for not equal.
`int operator != ( const Oid & lhs, const char *dotted_string);`	Compare an Oid & string for ! equal.
`int operator < ( const Oid &lhs, const Oid& rhs);`	Compare if less than an Oid.
`int operator < ( const Oid &lhs, const char *dotted_string);`	Compare if less than a string.
`int operator <=( const Oid &lhs, const Oid &rhs);`	Compare if less than or equal to an Oid.
`int operator <= ( const Oid &lhs, const char *dotted_string);`	Compare if less than or equal to a string.
`int operator > ( const Oid &lhs, const Oid &rhs);`	Compare if greater than an Oid.
`int operator > ( const Oid &lhs, const char * dotted_string);`	Compare if greater than a string.
`int operator >= ( const Oid&lhs, const Oid &rhs);`	Compare if greater than or equal to an Oid.
`int operator >= ( const Oid &lhs, const char*dotted_string);`	Compare if greater than or equal to a string.
`Oid& operator += ( const char *dotted_string);`	Append a string to an Oid.
`Oid& operator +=( const unsigned long i);`	Append a sub-id.
`Oid& operator+=( const Oid& oid);`	Append an Oid.
`unsigned long &operator [ ] (int position);`	Access sub-id value.

The Oid class supports a variety of member functions, shown in Table 6.3, for the display of object identifiers. These include displaying a partial or complete representation of an Oid.

Table 6.3   Oid Class Output Member Functions.

Output Member Functions	Description
`char * get_printable( const unsigned int n);`	Return the dotted format where n specifies how many subelements to include.
`char *get_printable( const unsigned long s,` `                     const unsigned long n);`	Return the dotted format where s specifies the start position and n specifies how many subelements to include.
`char *get_printable();`	Return the entire Oid as a dotted string.
`operator char *();`	Same as `get_printable()`.

The Oid class also supports a variety of member functions, shown in Table 6.4, that give you the ability to alter an Oid, determine its length, trim off data, compare portions of it to another Oid, and to determine an Oid's validity. The validity member function allows you to ask any Oid object whether it is valid or not. Validity is determined to be true if the Oid holds a valid ASN.1 object identifier that can be used.

Table 6.4   Oid Class Miscellaneous Member Functions.

Miscellaneous Member Functions	Description
`set_data ( const unsigned long *data,` `          const unsigned long n);`	Set the data of an Oid using a pointer and a length.
`unsigned long len( );`	Return the length, number of sub-elements, in an Oid.
`trim( const unsigned long n=1);`	Trim off the rightmost subelement of an Oid, default 1.
`nCompare( const unsigned long n,` `          const Oid& oid);`	Compare the first n sub-ids (left to right) of an Oid parameter.
`RnCompare( const unsigned long n,` `           const Oid& oid);`	Compare the last n sub-ids (right to left) of an Oid parameter.
`int valid( );`	Return the validity of an Oid.

Oid Class Examples

The examples that follow show the different ways in which the Oid class can be used. The code used in the example is ANSI/ISO C++ compatible. Example 6.1 constructs an Oid object, determines its validity, and prints it out.

Example 6.1   Constructing Oid Objects.

```
Oid oid("1.2.3.4.5.6.7");           // construct an Oid from a
                                    // dotted string
if (oid.valid()) {
   cout << "oid is valid\n";        // ::valid() determines validity
   cout << oid.get_printable();     // ::get_printable() prints out
                                    Oid

}
else
   cout << "oid is invalid";
```

Output
```
oid is valid
1.2.3.4.5.6.7
```

Example 6.2 constructs an array of five Oid objects, loads them up with values, and prints them out.

Example 6.2   Assignment of Oid Objects.

```
Oid oids[5];                        // construct an array of five oids
for (int x=0;x<5;x++) {
   if ( x>0)
      oids[x] += oids[x-1]          // overloaded [] and +=
   oids[x]+= x+1;
   // print them out
   cout << "oid[" << x<< "] = " <<oids[x].get_printable(); << "\n";
}
```

Output
```
oids[0] = 1
oids[1] = 1.2
oids[2] = 1.2.3
oids[3] = 1.2.3.4
oids[4] = 1.2.3.4.5
```

The Oid example shown in Example 6.3 creates an array of Oid objects and enables searching for specific Oid instances within the array.

Example 6.3 Searching an Array of Oid Objects.

```
#define BASEOID "1.3.6.1.2.1.1.3"
#define MAX 20

void oids_init( const Oid *oids) {    // initialize Oid objects
    for (int x=0;x<MAX;x++)   {
        oids[x] = BASEOID;  oids[x] += x+1;
    }
};

int oid_search( const Oid &oid, const Oid *oids) {
                                    // sequential search for Oid
    for (int x=0;x<MAX;x++)
        if ( oid == oids[x])
            return TRUE;
    return FALSE;
};

main() {                            // main
    Oid oid, oids[MAX];
    char input[80];

    oids_init( oids);              // initialize the Oids
    cout << "Enter an Oid?";
    cin >> input;
    oid = input;
    if ( !oid.valid())
        cout << "Invalid Oid!, try again";
    else
    if ( oid_search( oid, oids))
        cout << "\n" << oid.get_printable() << " Found";
    else
        cout << "\n" << oid.get_printable() << " Not Found";
}
```

Output
```
Enter an Oid? 1.3.6.1.2.1.1.3.2
1.3.6.1.2.1.1.3.2 Found

Enter an Oid? 1.3.6.1.2.1.1.5.1
1.3.6.1.2.1.1.3.2 Not Found
```

THE OCTET STRING CLASS

The SNMP++ Octet String class, OctetStr, gives programmers a way to use SMI octet strings easily and safely. When you use the octet class, it is no longer necessary to work with octets using internal pointers and lengths. When you use the SNMP++ OctetStr class, OctetStr objects can be easily instantiated, manipulated, and destroyed without the overhead of managing memory and memory leaks. Like the ANSI C++ string class, the OctetStr class supports a variety of ways to construct OctetStr objects, assign them, and use them with other SNMP++ classes. The OctetStr class is fully portable to any ANSI/ISO C++ environment. See Figure 6.2.

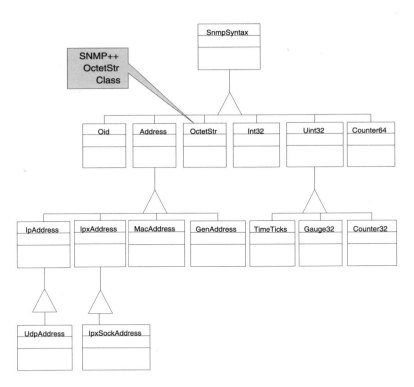

Figure 6.2   Object Modeling Technique (OMT) Object Model View of the SNMP++ OctetStr Class.

> ! The ASN.1 OCTET STRING object represents a sequence of octets (eight-bit bytes). These bytes can be used for storage of ASCII text or binary information.

SMI octet strings are a common MIB variable that enable the representation of printable ASCII strings and binary (non-printable) arrays of octets. The SNMP++ OctetStr supports a variety of ways to construct OctetStr objects. When dealing with ASCII strings, the OctetStr class can be thought of as a C++ string class with special features for SNMP.

An SNMP++ OctetStr object can be constructed in a variety of ways: with no data, with a null terminated string, with another OctetStr object, or with a pointer to some binary data. See Table 6.5.

Table 6.5   OctetStr Class Constructors and Destructor.

OctetStr Class Constructors and Destructor	Description
Constructors	
`OctetStr::OctetStr( void);`	Construct an OctetStr with no data.
`OctetStr::OctetStr( const char*string);`	Construct an OctetStr with a null terminated string.
`OctetStr::OctetStr( const unsigned char *s, unsigned long int i);`	Construct an OctetStr with a pointer and a length.
`OctetStr::OctetStr( const OctetStr &octet);`	Copy constructor.
Destructor	
`OctetStr::~OctetStr( );`	Destroy an OctetStr object.

A variety of member functions, shown in Table 6.6 on the next page, are provided to make using the OctetStr class useful and powerful. Of the member functions available, overloaded operators provide a natural look and feel when you are working with OctetStr objects.

Table 6.6   OctetStr Overloaded Operators.

OctetStr Class Member Functions	Description
Overloaded Operators	
`OctetStr& operator = ( const char * string);`	Assign an OctetStr object a null terminated string.
`OctetStr& operator = ( const OctetStr &octet);`	Assign an OctetStr to an OctetStr.
`int operator == ( const OctetStr &lhs,` `               const OctetStr &rhs);`	Compare two OctetStr objects for equivalence.
`int operator == ( const OctetStr &lhs,` `               const char * string);`	Compare an OctetStr and a char * for equivalence.
`int operator != ( const OctetStr &lhs,` `               const OctetStr &rhs);`	Compare two OctetStr objects for not equivalence.
`int operator != ( const OctetStr &lhs,` `               const char * string);`	Compare an OctetStr and a char * for not equivalence.
`int operator < ( const OctetStr &lhs,` `               const OctetStr &rhs);`	Test if one OctetStr is less than another.
`int operator < ( const OctetStr &lhs,` `               const char * string);`	Test if one OctetStr is less than a char *.
`int operator <= ( const OctetStr &lhs,` `               const OctetStr &rhs);`	Test if one OctetStr is less than or equal to another OctetStr.
`int operator <= ( const OctetStr &lhs,` `               const char * string);`	Test if one OctetStr is less than or equal to a char *.
`int operator > ( const OctetStr &lhs,` `               const OctetStr &rhs);`	Test if one OctetStr is greater than another OctetStr.
`int operator > ( const OctetStr &lhs,` `               const char * string);`	Test if one OctetStr is greater than a char *.
`int operator >= ( const OctetStr& lhs,` `               const OctetStr &rhs);`	Test if one OctetStr is greater than or equal to another OctetStr.
`int operator >= ( const OctetStr &lhs,` `               const char *);`	Test if one OctetStr is greater than or equal to a char *.

`OctetStr& operator +=( const char * string);`	Concatenate a string onto an OctetStr.
`OctetStr& operator +=( const unsigned char c);`	Concatenate a single `char` onto an OctetStr.
`OctetStr& operator+=( const OctetStr &octetstr);`	Concatenate an OctetStr object.
`unsigned char& operator[ ] ( int position i);`	Allow array-like access to an OctetStr.

The OctetStr class also supports a variety of member functions, shown in Table 6.7, that give you the ability to alter an OctetStr, determine its length, trim off data, compare portions to another OctetStr, and determine an OctetStr's validity. The validity member function enables you to ask any OctetStr object whether or not it is valid. Validity is determined to be true if the OctetStr holds a valid SMI octet string that can be used.

Table 6.7   OctetStr Miscellaneous.

Miscellaneous	Description
`void set_data( const unsigned char *s, unsigned long l);`	Set the data of an OctetStr using a pointer and length.
`int nCompare( const unsigned long n, const OctetStr &o);`	Compare n elements from parameter o.
`unsigned long len();`	Return the length of an OctetStr.
`int valid();`	Return the validity of an OctetStr.
`unsigned char * data();`	Return pointer to internal data.
`char * get_printable();`	Format for output, call hex dump if not ASCII.
`char * get_printable_hex();`	Format for output in hexadecimal format.

Special Features

When you print out an OctetStr object, the char * or
::get_printable() member functions automatically invoke the
::get_printable_hex() member function if the octet string contains
any character that is non-ASCII. This enables the user simply to cast the
OctetStr to a char * or call the ::get_printable() member function
and get nice output. The ::get_printable_hex() member function
formats the OctetStr in hexadecimal format.

OctetStr Class Examples

The examples that follow show the different ways in which the
OctetStr class can be used. Example 6.4 illustrates how an OctetStr may
be constructed.

Example 6.4   Construction and Use of an OctetStr Object.

```
OctetStr octetstr("YellowStone Cutthroat");
cout << octetstr.get_printable();
```

Output
```
YellowStone Cutthroat
```

Working with ASCII and Non-ASCII OctetStr Objects

When OctetStr objects contain all ASCII printable characters, they
can be printed out as such. If any non-ASCII character is present within
an OctetStr object, it can no longer be printed as an ASCII string.
Instead, a hexadecimal format is provided, as shown in Example 6.5.

Example 6.5   Printing an OctetStr Object.

```
OctetStr octetstr("Stonefly");
cout << octetstr.get_printable() << "\n";
octetstr[1]=3;
cout << octetstr.get_printable() << "\n";
```

Output
```
StoneFly
53 03 6F 6E 65 66 6C 79    S.onefly
```

Sorting an Array of OctetStr Objects   Example 6.6 creates an array of OctetStr objects, loads them up with data, sorts them, and finally prints them out.

Example 6.6   Sorting an Array of OctetStr Objects.

```
MAX 4
#define E10BT "Ethernet 10BaseT Hub"
#define E100BT "Ethernet 100BaseT Hub"
#define VG100 "100 VG/AnyLan Hub"
#define ATM "ATM Switch"

void init_octetstrs( OctetStr *octetstrs) {
                                    // initialize OctetStrs
   octetstrs[0] = E10BT; octetstrs[1] = E100BT;
   octetstrs[2] = VG100; octetstrs[3] = ATM;
};

void sort_octetstrs( OctetStr *octetstrs) {
                                    // sort the OctetStrs
   OctetStr temp;
   int y= MAX-1;
   while (y>0) {
   for ( int x=0;x<y;x++) {
      if (octetstrs[x+1] > octetstrs[x]) {
         temp = octetstrs[x]; octetstrs[x] = octetstrs[x+1];
                octetstrs[x]=temp;
      } y -=1;
   }
};
```

(continued)

Example 6.6 *(continued)*

```
void print_octetstrs( const OctetStr *octetstrs) {
                                    // print the OctetStrs
    for (int x=0;x<MAX;x++)
        cout << octetstrs[x].get_printable() << "\n";
};

main() {                                    // main
    OctetStr octetstrs[MAX];
    init_octetstrs( octetstrs);
    sort_octetstrs( octetstrs);
    print_octetstrs( octetstrs);
};
```

Output
```
ATM Switch
Ethernet 10BaseT Hub
Ethernet 100BaseT Hub
100 VG/AnyLan Hub
```

THE COUNTER32 CLASS

The SNMP++ Counter32 class provides benefits where SMI 32-bit counters are needed. SMI 32-bit counters are defined with the storage capabilities of an unsigned long integer. In addition to being unsigned long integers, SMI counters are treated as a distinct type. SMI counters are implemented in an agent such that a Counter32 object is used for accumulation or counting. Counter32 objects wrap when they reach a maximum value. For this reason, the SNMP++ Counter32 class has all the functionality and behavior of an unsigned long integer, but is a separate C++ class. Anything that can be done with an unsigned long integer can be done with an SNMP++ Counter32 object. The SMI Counter32 can be used in SNMP version 1 agents for all counting. The SMI Counter64 MIB object, available in SNMP version 2 only, is used where a Counter32 object would wrap too frequently. See Figure 6.3.

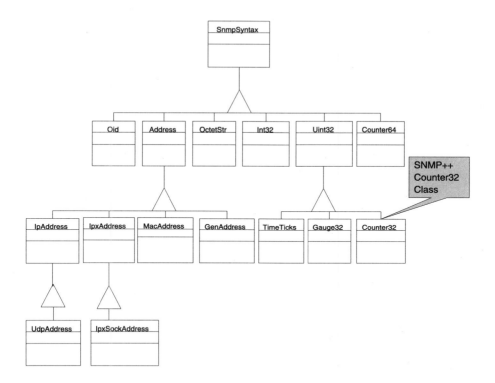

Figure 6.3 Object Modeling Technique (OMT) View of the SNMP++ Counter32 Class.

> The SMI Counter32 object represents a non-negative data type that monotonically increases. Upon receiving its maximum value, 2^32 -1, it wraps back to zero.

Since the SNMP++ Counter32 class is a subclass of the Uint32 class, it inherits the behavior and attributes of this parent class. In addition, Uint32 inherits from the SnmpSyntax class. This inheritance enables the reuse of all the virtual behavior of SnmpSyntax, such as the `::get_printable()` member function.

SNMP++ Counter32s can be constructed in a variety of ways, as shown in Table 6.8, including with no data, with an unsigned long integer, and with another Counter32.

Table 6.8   Counter32 Constructors and Destructor.

Counter32 Class Member Functions	Description
Constructors	
`Counter32::Counter32( void);`	Constructs an empty Counter32 object.
`Counter32::Counter32( const unsigned long i);`	Constructs a Counter32 object using an unsigned long integer.
`Counter32::Counter32( const Counter32 &c);`	Constructs a Counter32 object using another Counter32 object.
Destructor	
`Counter32::~Counter32( );`	Destroys a Counter32 object.

The Counter32 class supports two additional member functions, shown in Table 6.9. Because the Counter32 class has all the behavior of an unsigned long integer through Uint32, it does everything a unsigned long integer can do.

Table 6.9   Counter32 Overloaded Operators.

Overloaded Operators	Description
`Counter32& operator = ( const Counter32& c);`	Overloaded assignment operator.
`char * get_printable();`	Returns Counter32 formatted for output.
`operator unsigned long( );`	Gives unsigned long integer behavior.

Counter32 Class Examples

Counter32 can be used just as C unsigned integers can. This makes performing math easy. One might ask, then why use a separate class at all? Because a Counter32 is a distinct SMI value, it is not represented in a Management Information Base (MIB) as an unsigned long integer. For this reason, a distinct class is required so that when information is read or written from an MIB the desired Counter32 behavior is achieved.

Performing Simple Math with a Counter32 Object   Example 6.7 illustrates the use of Counter32 objects.

Example 6.7   Counter32 Construction and Destruction.

```
Counter32 counter32(12345);              // construct a Counter32
                                         // with a Uint32
counter32  = counter32 * counter32 / counter32;
                                         // behaves like a Uint32
cout << "Counter32 = " << counter32 << "\n";
```

Output
```
Counter32 = 12345
```

THE COUNTER64 CLASS

The SNMP++ 64-bit counter class enables the use of SMI 64-bit counters. 64-bit counters are defined as an SNMP version 2 SMI variable only. So, for SNMP version 1, this Management Information Base (MIB) variable does not exist. The Counter64 class enables easy use of 64-bit counters that are made up of two unsigned long portions (high and low). The Counter64 class provides overloaded operators for addition, subtraction, multiplication, and division, giving the Counter64 class a natural feel much like that of any other C numeric data type. Without a C++ class for Counter64s, programmers would be forced to use and manage the high and low portions manually, including taking care of math overflow and underflow. See Figure 6.4 on the next page.

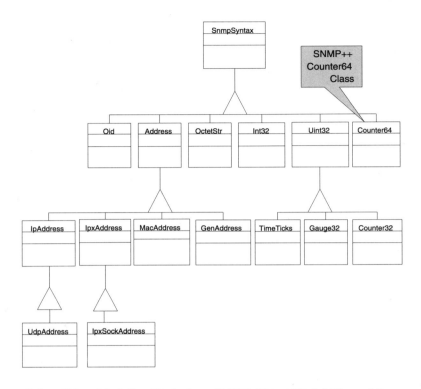

Figure 6.4   Object Modeling Technique (OMT) Object Model View of the
                 SNMP++ Counter64 Class.

   The Counter64 class is a subclass of the SnmpSyntax class, so it
inherits all the attributes and behavior from this parent. The Counter64
class supports a variety of constructors for the creation of Counter64
objects.

! The SMI Counter64 data type is an SNMP version 2 data type
with the same behavior as Counter32 but with twice the storage.
It increases monotonically until it reaches its maximum, $2^{64}-1$, then
wraps back to zero.

SNMP++ Counter64s can be constructed in a variety of manners, shown in Table 6.10, including with no data, with two unsigned integers, and with another Counter64.

Table 6.10   Counter64 Class Constructors and Destructor.

Counter64 Class Constructors and Destructor	Description
Constructors	
`Counter64::Counter64( void);`	Construct a Counter64 with no data.
`Counter64::Counter64( const unsigned long hi,` `                       const unsigned long low);`	Construct a Counter64 with two unsigned long integers.
`Counter64::Counter64( const Counter64 &ctr64);`	Copy Constructor.
`Counter64::Counter64( const unsigned long ul);`	Construct a Counter64 with a single unsigned long integer.
Destructor	
`Counter64::~Counter64( );`	Destroy an OctetStr object

In order to make the Counter64 class useful, it is required to support a variety of operators and member functions, thus giving it the look and feel of a normal C numeric data type. The overloaded operators allow for easy assignment, addition, subtraction, multiplication, and division. In addition, a set of useful conditional operators, shown in Table 6.11 on the next page, are included to provide for the comparison of Counter64s to other Counter64s, as well as to other C numeric data types.

Table 6.11   Counter64 Overloaded Operators.

Counter64 Class Member Functions	Description
Overloaded Operators	
`Counter64& operator = ( const Counter64 &ctr64);`	Assign a Counter64 to a Counter64.
`Counter64& operator = ( const unsigned long i );`	Assign a Counter64 an unsigned long integer, set low, clear high.
`Counter64 operator + ( const Counter64 &ctr64);`	Add two Counter64s.
`Counter64 operator - ( const Counter64 &ctr64);`	Subtract two Counter64s.
`Counter64 operator * ( const Counter64 &ctr64);`	Multiply two Counter64s.
`Counter64 operator / ( const Counter64 &ctr64);`	Divide two Counter64s.
`int operator == ( Counter64 &lhs, Counter64 &rhs);`	Test if two Counter64s are equal.
`int operator != ( Counter64 &lhs, Counter64 &rhs);`	Test if two Counter64s are not equal.
`int operator < ( Counter64 &lhs, Counter64 &rhs);`	Test if one Counter64 is less than another Counter64.
`int operator <= ( Counter64 &lhs, Counter64 &rhs);`	Test if one Counter64 is less than or equal to another Counter64.
`int operator > ( Counter64 &lhs, Counter64 &rhs);`	Test if one Counter64 is greater than another Counter64.
`int operator >= ( Counter64 &lhs, Counter64 &rhs);`	Test if one Counter64 is greater than or equal to another Counter64.

In addition to overloaded operators, a set of member functions, shown in Table 6.12, enable access to and modification of the high and low portions of a Counter64 object.

Table 6.12   Counter64 Member Functions.

Counter64 Member Functions	Description
unsigned long high();	Returns high portion.
unsigned long low();	Returns low portion.
void set_high();	Sets the high portion.
void set_low();	Sets the low portion.

THE GAUGE32 CLASS

The SNMP++ Gauge32 class provides benefits where SMI 32-bit gauges are needed. SMI gauges are defined with the storage capabilities of an unsigned long integer. In addition to being an unsigned long integer, SMI gauges are treated as a distinct type. For this reason, the SNMP++ Gauge32 class has all the functionality and behavior of an unsigned long integer but is a separate class. Anything that can be done with an unsigned long integer can be done with a Gauge32 object. See Figure 6.5 on the next page.

! The SMI Gauge32 object is represented by a non-negative integer that may increase or decrease in value. Upon reaching its maximum value, $2^{32} - 1$, it latches until its value decreases below $2^{32} - 1$.

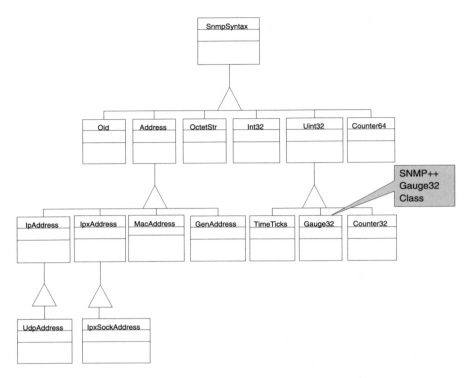

Figure 6.5   Object Modeling Technique (OMT) Object Model View of the SNMP++ Gauge32 Class.

Since the SNMP++ Gauge32 class is a subclass of the Uint32 class, it inherits the behavior and attributes of this parent class. In addition, Uint32 inherits from the SnmpSyntax class. This inheritance enables you to easily reuse of all the virtual behavior of SnmpSyntax, such as the `::get_printable()` member function.

SNMP++ Gauge32 objects can be constructed in a variety of ways, as shown in Table 6.13, including with no data, with an unsigned long integer, and with another Gauge32 object.

Table 6.13   Gauge32 Constructors and Destructor.

Gauge32 Class Member Functions	Description
Constructors	
`Gauge32::Gauge32( void);`	Constructs an empty Gauge32 object.
`Gauge32::Gauge32( const unsigned long i);`	Constructs a Gauge32 object using an unsigned long integer.
`Gauge32::Gauge32(  const Gauge32 &g);`	Constructs a Gauge32 object using another Gauge32 object.
Destructor	
`Gauge32::~Gauge32( );`	Destroys a Gauge32 object.

The Gauge32 class supports two additional member functions, shown in Table 6.14. Because the Gauge32 class has all the behavior of an unsigned long integer through Uint32, it can do everything a unsigned long integer can do.

Table 6.14   Gauge32 Overloaded Operators.

Overloaded Operators	Description
`Gauge32& operator = ( const Gauge32 &g);`	Overloaded assignment operator.
`char * get_printable();`	Returns formatted Gauge32 for output.
`operator unsigned long( );`	Gives unsigned long behavior.

Gauge32 Class Examples

Gauge32 can be used just like C unsigned integers. This makes performing math easy.

Performing Simple Math With a Gauge32 Object   Example 6.8 illustrates the use of Gauge32, including construction and output.

Example 6.8   Gauge32 Construction and Usage.

```
Gauge32 gauge32(12345);
gauge32 = gauge32 * gauge32 / gauge32;
cout << "Gauge32 = " << gauge32 << "\n";
```

Output
```
Gauge32 = 12345
```

THE TIMETICKS CLASS

The SNMP++ TimeTicks provides benefits where SMI timeticks are needed. SMI timeticks are defined with the storage capabilities of an unsigned long integer. In addition to being an unsigned long integer, SMI timeticks are treated as a distinct type. For this reason, the SNMP++ TimeTicks class has all the functionality and behavior of an unsigned long integer, but is a separate class. Anything that can be done with an unsigned long integer can be done with a TimeTicks object. SMI timeticks objects are represented and used in Management Information Bases (MIBs) where the storage of time is required. Keep in mind that this is a relative time based on some time epoch. This is typically the time since an agent was last rebooted. See Figure 6.6.

 The SMI TimeTicks object is represented using a non-negative integer that counts time in hundredths of a second.

SNMP++ TimeTicks objects can be constructed in a variety of ways, shown in Table 6.15, consistent with the Counter32 and Gauge32 objects.

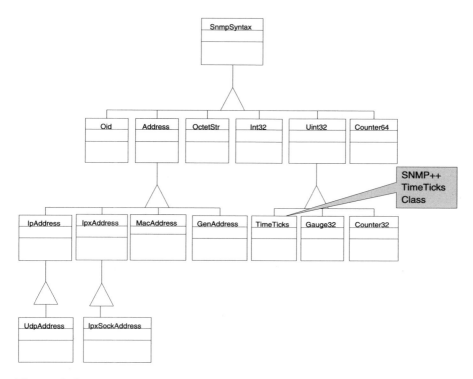

Figure 6.6 Object Modeling Technique (OMT) Object Model View of the SNMP++ TimeTicks Class.

Table 6.15 TimeTicks Class Constructors and Destructor.

TimeTicks Class Member Functions	Description
Constructors	
TimeTicks::TimeTicks(void);	Constructs an empty TimeTicks object.
TimeTicks::TimeTicks(const unsigned long i);	Constructs a TimeTicks object using an unsigned long integer.
TimeTicks::TimeTicks(const TimeTicks &t);	Constructs a TimeTicks object using another TimeTicks object.
Destructor	
TimeTicks::~TimeTicks( );	Destroys a TimeTicks object.

The TimeTicks class supports two additional member functions, shown in Table 6.16. Because the TimeTicks class has all the behavior of an unsigned long integer through Uint32, it can do everything a unsigned long integer can do.

Table 6.16   TimeTicks Class Overloaded Operators.

Overloaded Operators	Description
`TimeTicks& operator =( const TimeTicks&t);`	Overloaded assignment operator.
`char * get_printable();`	Formats for output, in the form DD Days, HH:MM:SS.hh.
`operator unsigned long();`	Gives unsigned long integer behavior to TimeTicks.

Special Features

When you print out a TimeTicks object using the function `TimeTicks::get_printable()`, the value is formatted automatically to a "DD days, HH:MM:SS.hh" format where DD is the number of days, HH is the number of hours (24-hour clock), MM is the minutes, SS is the seconds, and hh is the hundredths of a second. See Example 6.9.

Example 6.9   TimeTicks Example.

```
TimeTicks timeticks;                    // construct a TimeTicks

timeticks = 5000;
timeticks =  timeticks * 3600;

cout << "TimeTicks = " << timeticks.get_printable() << "/n";
```

Output
```
TimeTicks = 2 days, 2:00:00.0
```

THE NETWORK ADDRESS CLASSES

The Network Address class is a set of C++ classes that provide for simple, safe, portable, and efficient use of network addresses. Most network management applications require use of network addresses to access and manage devices. This includes address validation, modification, and user interface control. Rather than manage all the internal details of particular network addresses, the SNMP++ Network Address class encapsulates and hides the internal mechanisms, and frees the application programmer to focus on the problem at hand. See Figure 6.7.

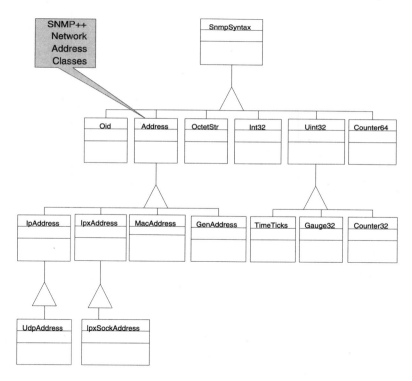

Figure 6.7   Object Modeling Technique (OMT) Object Model View of the
SNMP++ Address Class.

Using the Network Address Classes

The address class provides a number of benefits: automatic memory management, address validation, portability to any C++ environment, ease of use, and extensibility. Currently the Address class consists of six classes, the IpAddress Class, the UdpAddress Class, the IpxAddress Class, the IpxSockAddress Class, the MacAddress class, and the GenAddress class. In the future, other subclasses will be added including IP version 6.

Network Address Base Class

The address classes are based on one abstract class, the Address class. There may be no instances of this class. The Address class provides a consistent interface through the use of virtual member functions.

Address Classes Constructors

The base class, the Address class, is an abstract class. The class contains the commonality of all derived address classes. This includes an identical interface for constructing, accessing, and modifying Addresses. See Table 6.17.

Table 6.17   Address Classes Constructors.

Address Class Constructors	Description
IpAddress Class Constructors	
IpAddress::IpAddress(void);	Empty constructor.
IpAddress::IpAddress(const char *string);	Construct from a string, uses DNS.
IpAddress::IpAddress(const IpAddress &ipa);	Copy constructor.

UdpAddress Class Constructors

`UdpAddress::UdpAddress( void);`	Empty constructor.
`UdpAddress::UdpAddress( const char *string);`	Construct from a string, uses DNS.
`UdpAddress::UdpAddress( const  UdpAddress &udp);`	Copy constructor.

IpxAddress Class Constructors

`IpxAddress::IpxAddress( void);`	Empty constructor.
`IpxAddress::IpxAddress( const char *string);`	Construct from a string.
`IpxAddress::IpxAddress( const IpxAddress &ipxa);`	Copy constructor.

IpxSockAddress Class Constructors

`IpxSockAddress::IpxSockAddress( void);`	Empty constructor.
`IpxSockAddress::IpxSockAddress( const char *string);`	Construct from a string.
`IpxSockAddress::IpxSockAddress( const IpxSockAddress &ipxs);`	Copy constructor.

MacAddress Class Constructors

`MacAddress::MacAddress( void);`	Empty constructor.
`MacAddress::MacAddress( const char * string);`	Construct from a string.
`MacAddress::MacAddress( const  MacAddress &mac);`	Copy constructor.

GenAddress Class Constructors

`GenAddress::GenAddress( void);`	Empty constructor.
`GenAddress::GenAddress( const char * addr);`	Construct from a string.
`GenAddress::GenAddress( const GenAddress &addr);`	Copy constructor.

The Address class supports a variety of member functions, shown in Table 6.18 on the next page, to facilitate access and modification of Address objects. Included are overloaded operators for easy assignment and comparison of address objects.

Table 6.18   Common Address Class Member Functions.

Address Class Member Functions	Description
Common Member Functions, applicable to all Address classes	
`int operator == ( const Address &lhs,` `                   const Address &rhs);`	Determine if two Addresses are equal.
`int operator != ( const Address &lhs,` `                   const Address &rhs);`	Determine if two Addresses are not equal to another.
`int operator > ( const Address &lhs,` `                  const Address &rhs);`	Determine if one Address is greater than another.
`int operator >= ( const Address &lhs,` `                   const Address &rhs);`	Determine if one Address is greater than or equal.
`int operator < ( const Address &lhs,` `                  const Address &rhs);`	Determine if one Address is less than another.
`int operator<=( const Address &lhs,` `                 const Address &rhs);`	Determine if one Address is less than or equal to another.
`int operator == ( const Address &lhs,` `                   const char *inaddr);`	Determine if two Addresses are equal.
`int operator > ( const Address &lhs,` `                  const char *inaddr);`	Determine if an Address is greater than a string.
`int operator < ( const Address &lhs,` `                  const char *inaddr);`	Determine if an Address is less than a string.
`operator char * ( );`	Returns printable format.
`virtual int valid( );`	Determine if an Address is valid.
`unsigned char& operator[ ]( int position);`	Allow access to an Address object using array-like access.
`char * get_printable ( );`	Returns Address formatted for output.

In addition to the basic Address classes, two additional classes, shown in Table 6.19, are provided that should be used when IP address port numbers and IPX address socket numbers are required.

Table 6.19   Specific Address Class Member Functions.

Address Class Member Functions	Description
IPAddress Member Functions	
`char * friendly_name( int & status);`	Invoke DNS lookup for friendly name.
UdpAddress Member Functions	
`void UdpAddress:set_port( const unsigned int p);`	Set the port number for a UdpAddress object.
`unsigned int UdpAddress::get_port();`	Get the port number from a UdpAddress object.
IpxSockAddress Member Functions	
`IpxSockAddress::set_socket( const unsigned int s);`	Set the socket number from an IpxSockAddress.
`unsigned int IpxSocketAddress::get_socket();`	Get the socket number into an IpxSockAddress.

IpAddress Class Special Features

The IpAddress class will do an automatic Domain Name Services (DNS) lookup when it calls the `Address::get_printable()` member function. If the DNS is not active or if the address cannot be resolved, the dotted format is returned. Alternatively, an IpAddress can be constructed with a friendly name. In this case, the constructor invokes the DNS lookup. If the friendly name cannot be found, the address is invalid. This powerful feature enables you to utilize friendly names in your IpAddress user presentation.

GenAddress Class

The GenAddress class enables creation and use of generic addresses in circumstances where a GenAddress may take on the behavior and attributes of any of the other Address classes (IpAddress, UdpAddress, IpxAddress, IpxSockAddress, and MacAddress). When you work with arbitrary addresses, you can use a GenAddress. The constructor for the GenAddress class enables the creation of an Address with any character string. The constructor determines the specific type of Address that matches the string and thereafter gives the GenAddress the attributes and behavior of that Address. This saves the programmer from having to write code that deals explicitly with the differences across Addresses.

Example 6.10 shows how to construct GenAddress objects in a variety of ways.

Example 6.10   GenAddress Example.

```
GenAddress address1("10.4.8.5");              // make an IP GenAddress
GenAddress address2("01020304-10111213141516");  // make an IPX
                                             // GenAddress
GenAddress address3("01:02:03:04:05:06"); // make a MAC GenAddress

cout << address3.get_printable() << "\n"; // print out the
                                          // GenAddress

if ( !address1.valid())                      // check validity
    cout << "address1 ! valid";
else
    cout << "address 1 is valid";
```

Output
```
01:02:03:04:05:06
address 1 is valid
```

Address Class Validation

All address classes support the ::valid() member function. The ::valid() member function returns the validity of the particular Address object. Validation is determined when address objects are contructed or assigned. After assignment, the ::valid() member function can be used to determine validity. See Example 6.11.

Example 6.11   Address Validation.

```
MacAddress mac;
mac = "01.010a0d";                        // invalid MAC address
if ( !mac.valid())
    cout << "mac address is invalid";
```

Output
```
mac address is invalid
```

UdpAddresses and IpxSockAddresses

For most usage, users of SNMP++ utilize the well-known port and socket numbers for SNMP operations. For the Internet Protocol (IP) this includes using port 161 for an agent's destination port and port 162 for the trap/notification reception port. There are times when alternate port/socket specification is required. For these instances, the UdpAddress class and IpxSockAddress class allow definition of port or socket information.

Using UdpAddresses to Make Requests   When you request information from an agent that does not listen on the standard well-known port, you should use the `UdpAddress::set_port()` member function. The UdpAddress class supports two member functions to set and get custom port information. Attaching a UdpAddress to an SnmpTarget and using it for requests causes SNMP++ to utilize the custom port number.

Using IpxSockAddresses for Making Requests   When you request information from an agent that does not listen on the standard well-known IPX socket number, you should use the `IpxSockAddress::set_socket()` member function. The IpxSockAddress class supports two member functions to set and get custom socket number information. Attaching an IpxSockAddress to a Target and using it for requests causes SNMP++ to utilize the custom socket number.

Using UdpAddress and IpxSockAddress for Notification Reception UdpAddresses and IpxSockAddresses also can be used to specify alternate ports and sockets for notification reception. This enables applications to receive traps and informs on nonstandard ports and socket numbers.

Valid Address Formats

Valid Address formats are defined in Table 6.20.

Table 6.20   Valid Address Formats.

Address Class	Legal Format
IpAddress	X.X.X.X, where *X* is a number between 0 and 255.
Example	10.4.8.5
IpxAddress	XXXXXXXX*sep*XXXXXXXXXXXX where *X* is a hexadecimal number between 0 and F and *sep (separator)* can be a period (.) or colon (:) or dash (-).
Example	01020304.010203040506 aabbccdd:010203040506
MacAddress	XX:XX:XX:XX:XX:XX where *X* is a hexadecimal number between 0 and F.
Example	01:02:03:04:05:06
UdpAddress	X.X.X.X/Y where *X* is a number between 0 and 255, and *Y* specifies the port number where its value is between 0 and 9999.
Example	10.4.8.5/1052
IpxSockAddress	XXXXXXXX*sep*XXXXXXXXXXXX/Y where *X* is a hexadecimal number between 00 and FF and *sep (separator)* can be a period (.) or colon (:) or dash (-). *Y* specifies the port number where its value is between 0 and 9999.
Example	01020304-010203040506/2561

Address Class Examples

Example 6.12 shows a variety of features that can be accessed using the IpAddress class.

Example 6.12   IpAddress Examples.

```
IpAddress ip1("255.255.255.255");              // construct some
                                               // IpAddress objects
IpAddress ip2( ipaddress1);
ipAddress ip3;

cout << "ip1 = " << ip1.get_printable() << "\n";  // print them out
cout << "ip2 = " << ip2.get_printable() << "\n";
cout << "ip3 = " << ip3.get_printable() << "\n\n";

ip1 = "10.10.10.10";                           // reassign them
ip2 = ip1;
ip3 = (IpAddress) "1.1.1.1";

cout << "ip1 = " << ip1.get_printable() << "\n";  // print them out
                                                  // again
cout << "ip2 = " << ip2.get_printable() << "\n";
cout << "ip3 = " << ip3.get_printable() << "\n\n";

if ( ip1 <= ip2)
   cout << " ip1 <= ip2\n";
else
   cout << "ip1 > ip2\n";

cout << "ip1 friendly name = " << ip1.friendly_name() << "/n";
```

Output
```
ip1 = 255.255.255.255
ip2 = 255.255.255.255
ip3 =

ip1 = 10.10.10.10
ip2 = 10.10.10.10
ip3 = 1.1.1.1

ip1 <= ip2
ip1 friendly name = home
```

Example 6.13 shows a variety of features that can be accessed using the UdpAddress class.

Example 6.13   UdpAddress Examples.

```
UdpAddress udp1("255.255.255.255/160");          // construct some
                                                 // UdpAddress objects
UdpAddress udp2( ipaddress1);
UdpAddress udp3;

cout << "udp1 = " << udp1.get_printable() << "\n";   // print them out
cout << "udp2 = " << udp2.get_printable() << "\n";
cout << "udp3 = " << udp3.get_printable() << "\n\n";

udp1 = "10.10.10.10/162";                        // perform some
                                                 // reassignments
udp2 = ip1;
udp3 = (UdpAddress) "1.1.1.1";

cout << "udp1 = " << udp1.get_printable() << "\n";   // print them out
                                                     // again
cout << "udp2 = " << udp2.get_printable() << "\n";
cout << "udp3 = " << udp3.get_printable() << "\n\n";

if ( udp1 <= udp2)
   cout << " udp1 <= udp2\n";
else
   cout << "udp1 > udp2\n";

cout << "udp1 friendly name = " << udp1.friendly_name() << "/n";
```

Output
```
udp1 = 255.255.255.255/160
udp2 = 255.255.255.255/160
udp3 =

udp1 = 10.10.10.10/162
udp2 = 10.10.10.10/160
udp3 = 1.1.1.1/0

udp1 <= udp2
ip1 friendly name = home                 // allowed since UdpAddress is a
                                         // subclass of IpAddress
```

CHAPTER 7

The Variable Binding Class

An important data structure within SNMP is the Variable Binding. The Variable Binding (Vb) represents the binding of an object identifier and an associated value. Variable bindings are used within SNMP Protocol Data Units (PDUs) when information is exchanged between a manager and an agent. In SNMP++, the Variable Binding is encapsulated into a single class, the Vb class. See Figure 7.1 on the next page.

The Variable Binding (Vb) class consists of an Oid object and an SnmpSyntax object. In object-oriented methodology, this is simply a *has-a* relation. A Vb object *has an* Oid object and a SMI value. The Vb class enables the application programmer to instantiate Vb objects and to assign the Oid portion and value portions of an SNMP variable binding. Conversely, the Oid and value portions can be extracted. Variable binding lists in SNMP++ are represented as arrays of Vb objects. All SMI types are accommodated within the Vb Class. The Vb class provides full data hiding. The user does not need to know about SMI value types, Oid internal representations, or other related SNMP structures. The Vb class is fully portable using any standard ANSI C++ compiler.

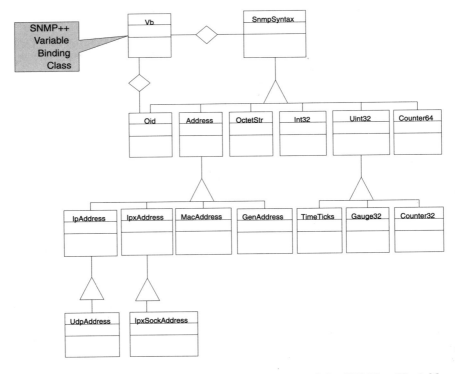

Figure 7.1   Object Modeling Technique (OMT) View of the SNMP++ Variable
Binding Class.

SNMP++ variable binding objects can be constructed in a variety of
ways, as shown in Table 7.1, including using other Vb and Oid objects.

Table 7.1   Vb Class Constructors and Destructor.

Variable Binding Class Member Functions	Description
Constructors	
`Vb::Vb( void);`	Construct an empty Vb object.
`Vb::Vb( const Oid &oid);`	Construct a Vb with an Oid portion.
`Vb::Vb( const Vb &vb);`	Copy constructor.
Destructor	
`Vb::~Vb();`	Destroy a Vb, free up all resources.

The Oid portion and the value portion of a Vb object can be accessed and modified using the member functions found in Table 7.2.

Table 7.2   Vb Class Member Functions.

Variable Binding Class Member Functions	Description
Set Oid/Get Oid	
`void set_oid( const Oid &oid);`	Set the Oid portion of a Vb.
`void get_oid( Oid &oid) const;`	Get the Oid portion.
Set Value	
`void set_value( const SMIValue &val);`	Set the value to any other SmiValue.
`void set_value( const int i);`	Set the value to an integer.
`void set_value( const long int i);`	Set the value to a long integer.
`void set_value( const unsigned long int i);`	Set the value to an unsigned long integer.
`void set_value( const char * ptr);`	Set the value to a null terminated string.
Get Value	
`int get_value( SMIValue &val);`	Get the value, use any SmiValue.
`int get_value( int &i);`	Get an integer value.
`int get_value( long int &i);`	Get an signed long integer.
`int get_value( unsigned long int &i);`	Get an unsigned long integer.
`int get_value( unsigned char * ptr, unsigned long &len);`	Get an unsigned char array, returns data and a len.
`int get_value( unsigned char * ptr, unsigned long &len, unsigned long maxlen);`	Get an unsigned char array and a len, up to max len in size.
`int get_value( char *ptr);`	Get a null terminated string.

(continued)

Table 7.2   *(continued)*

Variable Binding Class Member Functions	Description
Miscellaneous	
`SmiUINT32 get_syntax();`	Returns SMI syntax or SNMP v2 exception value.
`char *get_printable_value();`	Returns formatted value.
`char *get_printable_oid();`	Returns formatted Oid portion.
`void set_null();`	Sets a Vb object to hold a null value.
`int valid();`	Returns validity of a Vb.
Overloaded Operators	
`Vb& operator=( const Vb &vb);`	Assign one Vb to another.

VB CLASS PUBLIC MEMBER FUNCTIONS

The Vb class provides a variety of public member methods to access and modify Vb objects.

Vb Class Constructors and Destructors

A Vb object can be constructed with no arguments. In this case, shown in Example 7.1, the Oid and value portions must be set with subsequent member function calls.

Example 7.1   Creation of an Uninitialized Vb Object.

```
Vb myvb;        // construct a Vb object, myvb, which is uninitialized
```

Alternatively, a Vb object can be constructed with an Oid object as a construction parameter, as shown in Example 7.2. This initializes the Oid part of the Vb object to the Oid that was passed in. The Vb object makes a copy of the Oid that was passed in. This saves the programmer from having to worry about the duration of the parameter Oid.

Example 7.2   Creation of a Vb Object Using an Oid.

```
Oid oid("1.2.3.4.5.6");
Vb myvb( oid);
```

The destructor for a Vb object releases any memory and/or resources that were occupied. For statically defined objects, the destructor is called automatically when the object goes out of scope. Dynamically instantiated objects require usage of the delete construct to cause destruction.

Vb Class Get Oid/Set Oid Member Functions

The get and set Oid member functions enable you to get or set the Oid part of a Vb object. When you perform SNMP gets or sets, the variable is identified by setting the Oid value of the Vb via the `Vb::set_oid( const Oid oid)`. Conversely, the Oid portion can be extracted via the `Vb::get_oid( Oid &oid)` member function. The `get_oid()` member function is particularly useful when doing SNMP Get-Nexts.

The Oid portion of a Vb object can be set with an already constructed Oid object, as shown in Example 7.3 on the next page.

Example 7.3   Setting the Oid Portion of a Vb Object.

```
Oid oid("1.2.3.4.5.6");
Vb myvb;
myvb.set_oid( oid);
```

The Oid portion can be retrieved by providing a target Oid object, as shown in Example 7.4. This destroys the previous value of the Oid object.

Example 7.4   Getting the Oid Portion of a Vb Object.

```
Oid oid("1.2.3.4.5.6");
Vb myvb( oid);
Oid myoid;
myvb.get_oid( myoid);
cout << "myoid = " << myoid.get_printable() << "\n";
```

Output
```
myoid = 1.2.3.4.5.6
```

Vb Class Get Value/Set Value Member Functions

The get_value and set_value member functions enable you to get or set the value portion of a Vb object. These member functions are overloaded to provide for getting or setting different types. The internal hidden mechanisms of getting or setting Vb's handle all memory allocation/de-allocation. This frees the programmer from having to worry about SMI value structures and their management. The Vb::get_value() member functions typically are used to obtain a value of a Vb object after having performed an SNMP Get transaction. The Vb::set_value() member functions are useful when you wish to set values of Vbs when performing an SNMP Set transaction. In general, one may set or get any SnmpSyntax value in or from a Vb object.

Set an Integer   Setting the value portion of a Vb object to an integer is shown in Example 7.5. This maps to an SMI INT.

Example 7.5   Setting an Integer in a Vb Object.

```
int x = 25;
Vb myvb;
myvb.set_value( x );
```

Set an Unsigned Integer   Setting the value portion of a Vb object to a long integer is shown in Example 7.6. This maps to an SMI INT32.

Example 7.6   Setting an Unsigned Integer in a Vb Object.

```
long int y = 10128;
Vb myvb;
myvb.set_value( y );
```

Set an Unsigned Long Integer   Setting the value portion of a Vb object to an unsigned long integer is shown in Example 7.7. This maps to an SMI UNIT32.

Example 7.7   Setting an Unsigned Long Integer in a Vb Object.

```
unsigned long int w = 2055;
Vb myvb;
myvb.set_value( w );
```

Set a Gauge32   Setting the value portion of a Vb to a Gauge32 object is shown in Example 7.8. This maps to an SMI 32-bit gauge.

Example 7.8   Setting a Gauge32 SNMP++ Object in a Vb Object.

```
Gauge32 gauge32( 255);
Vb myvb;
myvb.set_value( gauge32);
```

Set a TimeTicks   Setting the value portion of a Vb object to a TimeTicks object is shown in Example 7.9. This maps to an SMI time ticks variable.

Example 7.9   Setting a TimeTicks SNMP++ Object in a Vb Object.

```
TimeTicks timeticks( 10042);
Vb myvb;
myvb.set_value( timeticks);
```

Set a Counter32   Setting the value portion of a Vb object to a Counter32 object is shown in Example 7.10. This maps to an SMI 32-bit counter.

Example 7.10   Setting a Counter32 SNMP++ Object in a Vb Object.

```
Counter32 counter32( 20044);
Vb myvb;
myvb.set_value( counter32);
```

Set a Counter64   Setting the value portion of a Vb object to a Counter64 object is shown in Example 7.11. This is used for SMI 64-bit counters comprised of a high and low 32-bit portion.

Example 7.11   Setting a Counter64 SNMP++ Object in a Vb Object.

```
Counter64 counter64( 1000,1000);
Vb myvb;
myvb.set_value( counter64);
```

Set an Oid   Setting the value portion of a Vb object to an Oid is shown in Example 7.12. In this case an Oid is used as the value. Note, this is not the same Oid used in the Vb Oid portion.

Example 7.12   Setting an Oid Object in the Value Portion of a Vb Object.

```
Oid oid("1.2.3.4.5.6");
Vb myvb;
myvb.set_value( oid);
```

Set a Character String   Setting the value portion of a Vb object to a char string is shown in Example 7.13. Really, this uses the SMI value portion of an octet string internally but makes it easier to use when it is an ASCII string (e.g., system descriptor).

Example 7.13   Setting a Null Terminated String in a Vb Object.

```
Vb myvb;
myvb.set_value("Pale Ale");
```

Set an IpAddress Setting the value portion of a Vb to an IP address object is shown in Example 7.14. This member function utilizes the SNMP++ Address class. IP address is an explicit SMI value type.

Example 7.14 Setting an IpAddress SNMP++ Object in a Vb Object.

```
IpAddress ipaddress("255.255.255.255");
Vb myvb;
myvb.set_value( ipaddress );
```

Set an IpxAddress Setting the value portion of a Vb to an IPX address object is shown in Example 7.15. This member function utilizes the Address class. IPX address is treated as an octet SMI value type.

Example 7.15 Setting an IpxAddress SNMP++ Object in a Vb Object.

```
IpxAddress ipxaddress("01020304:010203040506");
Vb myvb;
myvb.set_value( ipxaddress );
```

Set a MacAddress Setting the value portion of a Vb to an MAC address object is shown in Example 7.16. This member function utilizes the Address class. MAC address is treated as an octet SMI value type.

Example 7.16 Setting a MacAddress SNMP++ Object in a Vb Object.

```
MacAddress macaddress("01:02:03:04:05:06");
Vb myvb;
myvb.setvalue( macaddress );
```

Set a GenAddress   Setting a GenAddress object in a Vb is shown in Example 7.17. Here, the actual address type that the GenAddress is holding will be used to set the Vb value portion.

Example 7.17   Setting a GenAddress in a Vb Object.

```
GenAddress genaddress("255.255.255.255");
Vb myvb;
myvb.set_value( genaddress);
```

Set a UdpAddress   Setting an SNMP++ UdpAddress in a Vb object is shown in Example 7.18. The UdpAddress enables specification of an IpAddress and a port number.

Example 7.18   Setting a UdpAddress in a Vb Object.

```
UdpAddress udpaddress("255.255.255.255/167");
Vb myvb;
myvb.set_value( udpaddress);
```

Set an IpxSockAddress   Setting an SNMP++ IpxSockAddress object in a Vb object is shown in Example 7.19. The IpxSockAddress enables specification of an IpxAddress and a socket number (socket numbers are analogous to port numbers in IP).

Example 7.19   Setting an IpxSockAddress in a Vb Object.

```
IpxSockAddress ipxsockaddres("01020304:010203010203/248");
Vb myvb;
myvb.set_value( ipxsockaddress);
```

Set an OctetStr   Setting an SNMP++ OctetStr object in the value portion of a Vb object is shown in Example 7.20.

Example 7.20   Setting a OctetStr SNMP++ in a Vb Object.

```
OctetStr octetstr("Oatmeal Stout");
Vb myvb;
myvb.set_value( myvb);
```

Vb Class Get Value Member Functions

All `Vb::get_value()` member functions modify the parameter that is passed in. If a Vb object does not contain the requested parameter type, the parameter is not modified and an `SNMP_CLASS_INVALID` error status is returned. Otherwise, if successful, an `SNMP_CLASS_SUCCESS` error status is returned. Any subclass of the SnmpSyntax class can be retrieved from a Vb. SNMP version 2 introduced the notion of a variable binding exception in which a variable binding may have an error indicating that an individual variable binding in a Protocol Data Unit (PDU) was incorrect, while the remaining variable bindings are correct. In SNMP version 1, all variable bindings are required to be correct in order for the overall PDU status to be successful.

Getting an Integer   Getting and setting an integer value from a Vb object is shown in Example 7.21.

Example 7.21   Getting an Integer Value from a Vb Object.

```
int x= 5;
Vb myvb;
myvb.set_value( x);
int y;
myvb.get_value( y);
cout << "y = " << y;
```

Output
```
y = 5
```

Getting a Long Integer Setting and getting a long integer from a Vb object is shown in Example 7.22.

Example 7.22 Getting a Long Integer from a Vb Object.

```
long int y = 255;
Vb myvb;
myvb.set_value( y );
long int z;
myvb.get_value( z );
cout << " z = " << z;
```

Output
```
z = 255
```

Getting an Unsigned Long Integer Setting and getting an unsigned long integer value from a Vb object is shown in Example 7.23.

Example 7.23 Getting an Unsigned Long Integer from a Vb Object.

```
unsigned long y = 1024;
Vb myvb;
myvb.set_value( y );
unsigned long z;
myvb.get_value( z );
cout << " z = " << z;
```

Output
```
z = 1024
```

Getting a Gauge32 Setting and getting a Gauge32 SNMP++ object from a Vb object is shown in Example 7.24 on the next page.

Example 7.24   Getting a Gauge32 Object from a Vb Object.

```
Gauge32 x( 2048);
Vb myvb;
myvb.set_value( x);
Gauge32 y;
myvb.get_value( y);
cout << " y = " y.get_printable();
```

Output
```
y = 2048
```

Getting a TimeTicks   Getting a TimeTicks from a Vb object is shown in Example 7.25.

Example 7.25   Getting a TimeTicks Object from a Vb Object.

```
TimeTicks time1(4096);
Vb myvb;
myvb.set_value( time1);
TimeTicks time2;
myvb.get_value( time2);
cout << "time2 = " << time2.get_printable();
```

Output
```
time2 = 0:00:40.96
```

Getting a Counter32   Getting and setting a Counter32 from a Vb object is shown in Example 7.26.

Example 7.26   Getting a Counter32 Object from a Vb Object.

```
Counter32 x(1234);
Vb myvb;
myvb.set_value( x);
```

```
Counter32 y;
myvb.get_value( y);
cout << "y = "   << y;
```

Output
```
y = 1234
```

Getting an Oid   Getting an Oid object from a Vb object is shown in Example 7.27. Here, we are interested in getting the Oid value portion of the Vb.

Example 7.27   Getting an Oid from a Vb Object.

```
Oid x("1.2.3.4.5.6");
Vb myvb;
myvb.set_value( x);
Oid y;
myvb.get_value( y);
cout << "y = " << y.get_printable();
```

Output
```
y = 1.2.3.4.5.6
```

Getting an Unsigned Char Array   Getting an unsigned char string value from a Vb object is shown in Example 7.28 on the next page. Here, rather than grab an OctetStr SNMP++ object, we pass in a pointer and get back the modified memory and the length. Note, the caller in this case must ensure that sufficient memory is available or else memory corruption can occur. If you are not sure about the length, then perhaps the Vb::get_value (OctetStr octetstr) will suite your needs better.

Example 7.28   Getting an Unsigned Char Array from a Vb Object.

```
Vb myvb;
myvb.set_value( "OO SNMP");
unsigned char data[20];
unsigned int len;
myvb.get_data( data, len);
data[len]=0;
cout << "data = " << data;
```

Output
```
data = OO SNMP
```

Getting an OctetStr   Getting an OctetStr object from a Vb object is shown in Example 7.29. Using an OctetStr object, one can grab any octet string from a variable binding and not be concerned about the length. The OctetStr class automatically manages the length of a string for you.

Example 7.29   Getting an OctetStr from a Vb Object.

```
OctetStr x("Agent X");
Vb myvb;
myvb.set_value( x);
OctetStr y;
myvb.get_value( y);
cout << "y = " << y.get_printable();
```

Output
```
y = Agent X
```

Getting an IpAddress   Getting an IpAddress object from a Vb object is shown in Example 7.30. Because the SNMP++ IpAddress class maps to the SMI IP Address type, the Vb object treats it as an SMI IP address.

Example 7.30   Getting an IpAddress from a Vb Object.

```
IpAddress ip1("10.9.8.7");
Vb myvb;
myvb.set_value( ip1);
IpAddress ip2;
myvb.get_value( ip2);
cout << "ip2 = " << ip2.get_printable();
```

Output
```
ip2 = 10.9.8.7
```

Getting an IpxAddress   Getting an IPX address object from a Vb object is shown in Example 7.31. Because IPX addresses are not treated as a distinct SMI type, the Vb treats it internally as an octet string of length ten.

Example 7.31   Getting an IpxAddress from a Vb Object.

```
IpxAddress ipx1("01020304:010203040506");
Vb myvb;
myvb.set_value( ipx1);
IpxAddress ipx2;
myvb.get_value( ipx2);
cout << "ipx2 = " << ipx2.get_printable();
```

Output
```
ipx2 = 01020304:010203-040506
```

Getting a MacAddress   Getting a MacAddress object from a Vb object is shown in Example 7.32 on the next page. Because Ethernet MAC addresses are not treated as a distinct SMI type, the Vb will treat it internally as an octet string of length six.

Example 7.32   Getting a MacAddress from a Vb Object.

```
MacAddress mac1("01:02:03:04:05:06");
Vb myvb;
myvb.set_value( mac1);
MacAddress mac2;
myvb.get_value( mac2);
cout << "mac2 = " << mac2.get_printable();
```

Output
```
mac2 = 01:02:03:04:05:06
```

Getting a GenAddress   Getting a GenAddress object from a Vb object is shown in Example 7.33. Because an SNMP++ GenAddress is represented internally as one of the derived Address classes (IpAddress, UdpAddress, IpxAddress, IpxSockAddress, MacAddress), the Vb treats it as it really is.

Example 7.33   Getting a GenAddress from a Vb Object.

```
IpAddress ip1("255.254.253.252);
Vb myvb;
myvb.set_value( ip1);
GenAddress gen1;
myvb.get_value( gen1);
cout << "gen1 = " << gen1.get_printable();
```

Output
```
gen1 = 255.254.253.252
```

Getting a UdpAddress   Getting a UdpAddress object from a Vb object is shown in Example 7.34. UdpAddress is treated as an SMI octet string of length six, two bytes for the port number.

Example 7.34   Getting a UdpAddress from a Vb Object.

```
GenAddress gen1("10.10.10.10/160");
Vb myvb;
myvb.set_value( gen1);
UdpAddress udp1;
myvb.get_value( udp1);
cout << "udp1 = " << udp1.get_printable();
```

Output
```
udp1 = 10.10.10.10/160
```

Getting an IpxSockAddress   Getting an IpxSockAddress object from a Vb object is shown in Example 7.35. IpxSockAddress is defined as an Address object.

Example 7.35   Getting an IpxSockAddress from a Vb Object.

```
GenAddress gen1("01020304:010203040506/123");
Vb myvb;
myvb.set_value( gen1);
IpxSockAddress ipxsock1;
myvb.get_value( ipxsock1);
cout << "ipxsock1 = " << ipxsock1.get_printable();
```

Output
```
ipxsock1 = 01020304:010203-040506/123
```

Vb Object Validation Check

You can check an instantiated Vb object to determine if it is valid by invoking the Vb::valid() member function, as shown in Example 7.36 on the next page. Valid Vbs are those that have been assigned an Oid.

Example 7.36   Validation of a Vb Object.

```
Vb myvb;
if (!myvb.valid())
    cout << "myvb is invalid since it has no Oid portion";
```

Output
```
myvb is invalid since it has no Oid portion
```

Printing the Oid and Value Portions of a Vb Directly

The Vb class supports two member functions for printing out the Oid and value portions of a Vb object directly without having to extract the Oid and SnmpSyntax objects and then print them out. These functions are particularly handy when dumping the contents of a PDU. See Example 7.37.

Example 7.37   Printing Out Vb Oid and Value Directly.

```
Vb myvb;
myvb.set_oid( (Oid) "1.2.3.4.5.6");
myvb.set_value( (IpAddress) "10.4.8.5");
cout << "myvb Oid = "<< myvb.get_printable_oid() << "\n";
cout << "myvb Value = " << myvb.get_printable_value();
```

Output
```
myvb Oid = 1.2.3.4.5.6
myvb Value = 10.4.8.5
```

Vb Object Assignment to Other Vb Objects

Vb objects can be assigned to one another using the overloaded assignment operator, =. This allows for the easy assignment of one Vb object to another without having to interrogate a Vb object for its contents and then assign them manually to the target Vb object. See Example 7.38.

Example 7.38   Assignment of a Vb to a Vb.

```
Vb vb1;
vb1.set_value( (Oid) "1.2.3.4.5.6");
vb1.set_value( (int) 36);
Vb vb2;
vb2 = vb1;
cout << "vb2 Oid = " << vb2.get_printable_oid() << "\n";
cout << "vb2 Value = " << vb2.get_printable_value();
```

Output
```
vb2 Oid = 1.2.3.4.5.6
vb2 Value = 36
```

Vb Object Errors

When you get data from a variable binding object, using Vb::get_value(), an error can occur based on the value of the Vb and the type of value you have requested. (See Table 7.3.) For example, assume a Vb object has an OctetStr and you are trying to get a TimeTicks object out of it. The Vb::get_value() will fail because a TimeTicks object cannot be returned. In the event an error occurs, the caller can use Vb::get_syntax() to interrogate the Vb for its actual value or exception value.

Table 7.3   Vb::get_value() Member Function Return Codes.

Vb::get_value() return value	Description
SNMP_CLASS_SUCCESS	Success, requested value was returned.
SNMP_CLASS_INVALID	Error, Vb value does not hold requested value.

Vb Syntax and Exception Values

In the event a `Vb::get_value()` member function fails, it may be due to a Variable Binding exception. Vb exceptions, defined for SNMP version 2, allow Vb errors to occur while the remaining Vbs within a PDU are still valid. Vb exceptions can be detected in SNMP++ using the `Vb::get_syntax()` member function. (See Table 7.4.) The `Vb::get_syntax()` member function returns the SMI syntax of the value currently held by a Vb object. It also returns the Vb exception value in the event one has occurred.

Table 7.4   Vb Syntax and Exception Values.

`Vb ::get_syntax()` Return Value	Description
SNMP_SYNTAX_OCTETS	Vb object holds an OctetStr object.
SNMP_SYNTAX_NULL	Vb object holds nothing.
SNMP_SYNTAX_OID	Vb object holds an Oid object.
SNMP_SYNTAX_INT32	Vb object holds a 32-bit integer.
SNMP_SYNTAX_IPADDR	Vb object holds an IP address.
SNMP_SYNTAX_CNTR32	Vb object holds a Counter32 object.
SNMP_SYNTAX_GAUGE32	Vb object holds a Gauge32 object.
SNMP_SYNTAX_TIMETICKS	Vb object holds a TimeTicks object.
SNMP_SYNTAX_CNTR64	Vb object holds a Counter64 object.
SNMP_SYNTAX_UINT32	Vb object holds an unsigned 32-bit integer.
Vb Exception Values	
SNMP_SYNTAX_NOSUCHOBJECT	Requested object does not exist in MIB.
SNMP_SYNTAX_NOSUCHINSTANCE	Instance of object does not exist in MIB.
SNMP_SYNTAX_ENDOFMIBVIEW	End of MIB reached.

CHAPTER 8

The Protocol Data Unit
and SnmpTarget Classes

$\mathbf{T}$he previous chapters in this part described various components of SNMP++, including the SnmpSyntax classes and the Variable Binding class. This chapter puts all the basic SNMP++ pieces together into two main classes that are used for communication with agents. Described here are the Protocol Data Unit class and the SnmpTarget class. In the chapters that follow, the Pdu class and SnmpTarget class are used extensively for all interaction with agents and MIBs.

THE PDU CLASS

The SNMP++ Pdu class is the C++ encapsulation of the SNMP Protocol Data Unit (PDU). PDUs are the basic means of SNMP communication between a manager and an agent. All SNMP transactions involve the use of PDUs because they contain the data being requested or modified. SNMP++ makes working with PDUs easy and safe through use of the Pdu class. See Figure 8.1 on the next page.

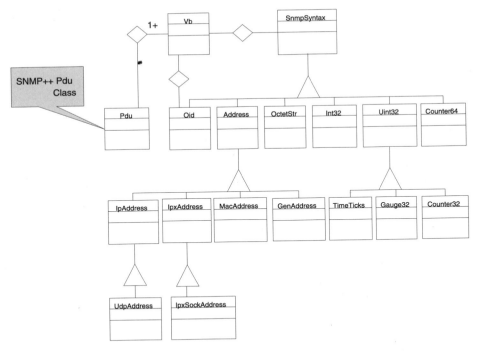

Figure 8.1   Object Modeling Technique (OMT) View of the SNMP++ Protocol
Data Unit Class.

The Pdu class allows easy construction, destruction, Vb object loading, and unloading of Pdu objects. Because SNMP++ is a bilingual API,
the Pdu class does not contain information specific to SNMP version 1 or
version 2. The Pdu class can be used for all Snmp class request member
functions. The Pdu class is used to interface with the Snmp class for
SNMP requests and is also used as a callback parameter for asynchronous requests and notification reception.

For the most part, all Pdu objects are the same in SNMP++. That is,
all Pdu objects have identical attributes. The only exception is when Pdu
objects are used for sending notifications, traps, and informs. For notifications, three additional Pdu class member functions can be used to set
the identity, timestamp, and enterprise.

Pdu Class Constructors and Destructors

SNMP++ Pdu objects can be constructed in a variety of ways, as shown in Table 8.1, including the construction of an empty Pdu using Vb objects and other Pdu objects.

Table 8.1   Pdu Class Constructors and Destructor.

Pdu Class Member Functions	Description
Constructors	
`Pdu::Pdu( void);`	Construct an empty Pdu.
`Pdu::Pdu( Vb* pvbs,` `          const int pvb_count);`	Construct a Pdu with an array of Vbs and size.
`Pdu::Pdu( const Pdu &pdu);`	Construct a Pdu with another Pdu.
Destructor	
`Pdu::~Pdu();`	Destructor, frees all memory held.

There are a variety of ways to construct Pdu objects, including both with and without construction parameters. Pdu destruction handles the de-allocation of all memory held by the Pdu including the variable binding list. See Example 8.1.

Example 8.1   Construction of Pdu Objects.

```
Pdu pdu1;                      // construct an empty Pdu object
Vb myvbs[5];                   // construct some Vb objects
Pdu pdu2( (Vb*) myvbs, 5);     // make another Pdu using the Vbs
Pdu pdu3( pdu2);               // make a third Pdu using second
                               // Pdu
```

Pdu Class Access Member Functions

The Pdu class supports a variety of member functions to get and set Pdu member variables, as shown in Table 8.2. Included in the class are ways to get and set the variable bindings, error information, request identification, and type information.

Table 8.2   Pdu Class Member Functions.

Pdu Class Member Functions	Description
`int get_vblist( Vb* pvbs,` `            const int pvb_count);`	Copies Vbs to caller parameters.
`int set_vblist( Vb* pvbs,` `            const int pvb_count);`	Sets callers Vbs in the Pdu.
`int get_vb( Vb &vb, const int index);`	Get a particular Vb from a Pdu.
`int set_vb( Vb &vb, const int index);`	Set a particular Vb in a Vb.
`int get_vb_count();`	Get the Vb count from a Pdu.
`int get_error_status();`	Get the error status from a Pdu.
`int get_error_index();`	Get the error index from a Pdu.
`unsigned long get_request_id();`	Get the request id from a Pdu.
`unsigned short get_type();`	Get the Pdu type.
`int valid();`	Is the Pdu valid?
`int delete_vb( const int position);`	Removes Vb at specified position in Pdu.
`int trim(const int i=1);`	Trim off the last Vb in the Pdu, default 1.

SNMP++ Pdu objects can be loaded and unloaded with Vb objects. (See Example 8.2.) This is required for all SNMP transactions. A Pdu object can be thought of as an ordered collection of Vbs plus a few other attributes pertinent to SNMP Protocol Data Units (PDUs). The Pdu object maintains its own copy of Vbs so that once a Vb object has been placed in a Pdu object, the original Vb need no longer remain in scope.

Example 8.2   Loading and Unloading Vbs from Pdus.

```
Vb vbs_in[2];
vbs_in[0].set_oid("1.3.6.1.2.1.1.1.0");    // system descriptor
                                           // object
vbs_in[1].set_oid("1.3.6.1.2.1.1.2.0");    // system object id
Pdu pdu;
pdu.set_vb_list( (Vb*) vbs_in,2);          // place the Vbs into
                                           // the Pdu
Vbs vbs_out[2];
pdu.get_vbs( (Vb*) vbs_out,2);             // extract the Vbs
                                           // out of the Pdu
cout << vbs_out[0].get_printable_oid() << "\n";
cout << vbs_out[0].get_printable_oid() << "\n";
```

Output
```
1.3.6.1.2.1.1.1.0
1.3.6.1.2.1.1.2.0
```

Along with the Vbs, a Pdu maintains a few other important attributes that reflect its error state. Member functions are provided to obtain the number of Vbs in the Pdu, the SNMP error status, the SNMP error index, the request identifier, and the type of PDU. Most of these values are available after a Pdu has "been on the wire" or has been used for an SNMP transaction.

Determination of Pdu Error Status   Included within every Pdu object is an error status indicator that is used for error designation within a Pdu. This error status maps directly to the SNMP standard SMI PDU error status values found within RFC 1905 [SNMP RFCs]. Table 8.3 on the next page shows possible errors that can be returned as a result of Pdu::get_error_status().

Table 8.3   Pdu Error Status Values.

Pdu Error Status Macro	Value	Description
SNMP_ERROR_TOO_BIG	1	Pdu Too Big, see error index.
SNMP_ERROR_NO_SUCH_NAME	2	No Such Variable Binding name, see returned error index.
SNMP_ERROR_BAD_VALUE	3	Bad Variable Binding Value, see returned error index.
SNMP_ERROR_READ_ONLY	4	Variable Binding is read only, see returned error index.
SNMP_ERROR_GENERAL_VB_ERR	5	General Variable Binding error, see returned error index.
SNMP_ERROR_NO_ACCESS	6	Operation Failure, No Access.
SNMP_ERROR_WRONG_TYPE	7	Operation Failure, Bad Type.
SNMP_ERROR_WRONG_LENGTH	8	Operation Failure, Bad Length.
SNMP_ERROR_WRONG_ENCODING	9	Operation Failure, Wrong Encoding.
SNMP_ERROR_WRONG_VALUE	10	Operation Failure, Wrong Value.
SNMP_ERROR_NO_CREATION	11	Operation Failure, No Creation.
SNMP_ERROR_INCONSIST_VAL	12	Operation Failure, Inconsistent Value.
SNMP_ERROR_RESOURCE_UNAVAIL	13	Operation Failure, Resource Unavailable.
SNMP_ERROR_COMITFAIL	14	Operation Failure, Commit Failure.
SNMP_ERROR_UNDO_FAIL	15	Operation Failure, Undo Failure.
SNMP_ERROR_AUTH_ERR	16	Operation Failure, Authorization Error.
SNMP_ERROR_NOT_WRITEABLE	17	Operation Fail, Not Writeable.
SNMP_ERROR_INCONSIS_NAME	18	Operation Failure, Inconsistent Name.

Determination of Pdu Error Index In the event the Pdu error status is set and the error applies to a particular Variable Binding, the error index value is used to index the Variable Binding in error.

! All SNMP++ arrays and containers are indexed by base zero. That is, given a list of Vbs in a Pdu the first Vb is Vb #0. This is consistent with arrays in C and C++. There is one value found in SNMP that is one-based, however. This value is the error index of an ASN.1 PDU. The `Pdu::get_error_index()` member function returns a one-based index. Why? The original design of SNMP was non-language-specific. The notion of zero-based arrays is exclusive to C and C++.

Working with Pdu Request Identifiers One other important attribute of a Pdu is the request identifier. The request identifier is used to differentiate one Pdu from another as they move from machine to machine. For the most part, when SNMP++ is used a user does not have to be concerned with request ids. The SNMP++ API takes care of automatically assigning and managing the request ids for you. If for some reason you want to access a Pdu request id, the member function `Pdu::get_request_id()` is provided for you to do so. See Example 8.3.

Example 8.3   Accessing Pdu Error Information.

```
// assume that we have a Pdu which represents a response PDU
cout << "pdu vb count = " << pdu.get_vb_count() << "\n";
cout << "pdu error status =" << pdu.get_error_status() << "\n";
cout << "pdu error index =" << pdu.get_error_index() << "\n";
cout << "pdu request id = " << pdu.get-request_id() << "\n";
```

Output
```
pdu vb count = 5
pdu error status = 0
pdu error index = 0
pdu request id = 2331
```

Pdu Class Overloaded Operators

The Pdu class supports overloaded operators, as shown in Table 8.4, for assignment and concatenation of Vb objects to a Pdu. See Example 8.4 for a demonstration.

Table 8.4   Pdu Class Overloaded Operators.

Pdu Class Overloaded Operators	Description
`Pdu& operator=( const Pdu &pdu);`	Assign one Pdu to another.
`Pdu& operator+=( Vb &vb);`	Append a Vb to a Pdu.

Example 8.4   Overloaded Pdu Operators.

```
Pdu pdu1;
Vb vb;
vb.set_oid("1.3.6.1.2.1.1.1.0");
pdu += vb;
Pdu pdu2;
pdu2.get_vb( vb,0);
cout << "pdu2's vb, oid portion = " << vb.get_printable_oid();
```

Output
```
pdu2's vb, oid portion =  1.3.6.1.2.1.1.1.0
```

Pdu Class Member Functions for Traps and Informs

When working with notifications and trap and inform PDUs, SNMP++ provides member functions to get and set notification values from Pdu objects. (See Table 8.5.) Such PDUs have a few additional attributes, including a timestamp, an identifier, and an enterprise. The timestamp of an SNMP++ notification Pdu is represented using the SNMP++ TimeTicks object. This represents the time when the notification was sent. The notification identifier is represented using an Oid object. This Oid is commonly referred to as a *trap id*. There are a variety of notification ids including those representing standard traps and those representing vendor-specific traps. Since SNMP++ provides an SNMP version 2 view of the world, there is no concept of a generic and specific value of a trap. Instead, a single Oid is used. The last attribute of an SNMP++ notification Pdu is the enterprise; it is also represented using an Oid object. For more on notifications and their usage, please refer to the SNMP++ Snmp class, and the `Snmp::trap()` member function.

Table 8.5   Member Functions for Notification Pdus.

Member Functions for Pdu Class Inform and Trap Usage	Description
`void set_notify_timestamp( const TimeTicks & timestamp);`	Set timestamp on a trap or inform Pdu.
`void get_notify_timestamp( TimeTicks & timestamp);`	Get the timestamp from a trap or inform Pdu object.
`void set_notify_id( const Oid id);`	Set the ID on a trap or inform Pdu.
`void get_notify_id( Oid &id);`	Get the ID from a trap or inform Pdu.
`void set_notify_enterprise( const Oid & enterprise);`	Set the enterprise ID on a trap or inform Pdu.
`void get_notify_enterprise( Oid & enterprise);`	Get the enterprise ID on a trap or inform Pdu.

THE SNMPTARGET CLASS

The SnmpTarget class is a C++ class used with SNMP++ to enable the definition and usage of targets. A target can be thought of as a management definition of an agent that is to be used for SNMP communication. A target consists of more than just a network address. SnmpTargets contain retransmission and time-out policy information, the SNMP protocol type (SNMP version 1 or version 2), and more. The CTarget, community-based target, is defined as a subclass of the abstract SnmpTarget class. The CTarget class may be used for SNMP version 1 and version 2 communication. Community-based SNMP utilizes community names for access to agents. The SnmpTarget class enables an SNMP++ session to be independent of a particular agent's attributes. Other APIs tie the agents attributes to a session. This forces one to have a session for each managed target or to change the session attributes with each request. The SnmpTarget class enables sessions and targets to remain independent and, as will be shown, to make things cleaner and easier. See Figure 8.2.

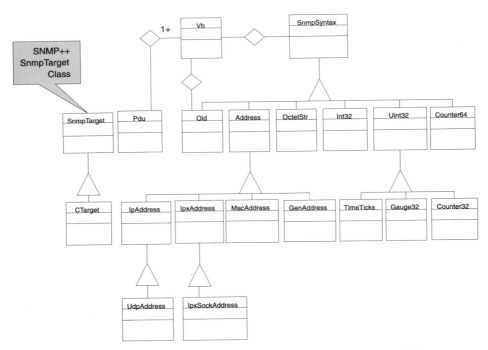

Figure 8.2   Object Modeling Technique (OMT) Object Model View of the SNMP++ SnmpTarget Class.

Abstract Targets

SNMP++ supports the notion of an abstract target. All SNMP++ member functions that use targets accept abstract targets, SnmpTargets, and not just specific derived target objects. This abstract interface allows minimal code change when supporting new SnmpTargets. Currently SNMP++ supports community-based targets. As the IETF works on and approves secure SNMP, newly derived targets for SNMP++ can be introduced.

Target Addresses

Each SnmpTarget has associated with it an SNMP++ Address object. This Address is a GenAddress and, therefore, may take the value of any SNMP++ Address (IP, IPX, or whatever). To specify the address of a managed agent, the agent's address simply is specified and then is attached to a Target via construction parameters or through member functions.

Retransmission Policies

Each SnmpTarget has a retransmission policy in which a defined time-out and retry specify how long to wait for an SNMP response and how many times to retry if an SNMP response is not received by the SNMP++ protocol engine. Time-outs are defined in hundredths of a second where a value of 100 means wait one second for each response. Retries denote the number of times to retry where the first request is not a retry, it is just a try. So a retry value of three (3) equates to retry a maximum of three times when waiting for responses. The total amount of time to wait can be computed as follows:

```
Wait Time = time-out * (retry+1)
```

If an SNMP++ response does not arrive in the computed total wait time, an SNMP++ time-out error code is returned. This behavior applies to both blocked and asynchronous calls. Table 8.6 shows member functions pertaining to time-outs and retries.

Table 8.6   Member Functions That Apply to All SnmpTargets.

SnmpTarget Abstract Class Member Functions	Description
`int valid();`	Returns validity of an SnmpTarget.
`void set_retry( const int r);`	Set the retry value.
`int get_retry();`	Get the retry value.
`void set_timeout( const unsigned long t);`	Set the time-out value.
`unsigned long get_timeout();`	Get the time-out value.

CTarget Class (Community-Based Targets)

The CTarget class enables the explicit definition of community-based targets. A CTarget defines an SNMP agent using SNMP community-based attributes. This includes the *read* and *write community names* and a network address. The CTarget class should be used when the application programmer knows explicitly that the agent supports SNMP community-based access (IETF SNMP version 1 or version 2c). See Table 8.7.

Table 8.7   CTarget Constructors.

CTarget Class Constructors	Description
`CTarget::CTarget( void);`	Construct an invalid CTarget. Defaults to "public" for community names and retry=1, time-out=100ms for retransmission policy.

`CTarget::CTarget( const Address &address,`
`              const char *read_community,`
`              const char *write_community);`
	Construct a CTarget using community names and an Address object. Defaults to retry=1 and time-out =100ms for retransmission policy.

`CTarget( const Address &address,`
`       const OctetStr &read_community,`
`       const OctetStr &write_community);`
	Construct a CTarget using OctetStr Communities and an Address.

`CTarget::CTarget( Address &address);`	Construct a CTarget using an Address object. Defaults to "public" for community names and retry=1, time-out=100ms for retransmission policy.
`CTarget::CTarget( const CTarget &target);`	Copy constructor.

Constructing CTarget Objects

CTarget objects may be instantiated in three different ways, as shown in Example 8.5.

Example 8.5   Constructing CTarget Objects.

```
// valid complete instantiation
CTarget   target((IpAddress)"10.10.10.10",// Address
               "public",                  // read community name
               "public");                 // write community name

// valid complete using "public" defaults
CTarget target((IpAddress) "1.2.3.4");

// invalid CTarget, doesn't have an address yet
CTarget target;
```

The CTarget class supports a variety of member functions, as shown in Table 8.8 on the next page, to access and modify community names. Since, CTarget represents both SNMP version 1 and version 2 SnmpTargets, one additional member function is present to get and set the version of SNMP to utilize. All SNMP++ access member functions support a bilingual interface so that when SNMP information is accessed the identical interface can be used to access SNMP version 1 or version 2 information. By default when a CTarget is created, the version is set to SNMP version 1.

Table 8.8   CTarget Member Functions.

CTarget Member Functions	Description
`char * get_readcommunity();`	Returns read community name.
`void get_readcommunity( OctetStr` `                    &community);`	Get the read community as OctetStr.
`void set_readcommunity( const char *` `                    community);`	Set the read community.
`void set_readcommunity( const OctetStr` `                    &community);`	Set the read community name using an OctetStr.
`char * get_writecommunity();`	Get the write community.
`void get_writecommunity( OctetStr` `                     &community);`	Get the write community as an OctetStr.
`void set_writecommunity( const char *` `                     community);`	Set the write community.
`void set_writecommunity( const community);`	Set the write community using an OctetStr.
`int  get_address( GenAddress & address);`	Get the Address object.
`void set_address( Address & address);`	Set the Address portion.
`CTarget& operator=( const CTarget` `                &target);`	Assign one CTarget to another.
`snmp_version get_version();`	Return the SNMP version. (version1 or version2c)
`void set_version( const snmp_version v);`	Set the version. (version1 or version2c)
`int operator==( const CTarget &lhs,` `                const CTarget &rhs);`	Compare two CTargets.

Modifying and Displaying CTarget Objects   Once a CTarget object is created, the retransmission policy information and community name information can be modified, as shown in Example 8.6.

Example 8.6   Modifying and Displaying CTarget Objects.

```
CTarget target( (IpAddress) "10.4.8.5");
target.set_readcommunity("private");    // modifies the read community
target.set_writecommunity("private");   // modifies the write community
target.set_address( (IpAddress) "15.29.33.210");
cout << "Target write community = " << target.get_writecommunity()
                                    << "\n";
cout << "Target read community = " << ct.get_readcommunity() << "\n";
GenAddress address;
target.get_address( address);
cout << "Target address = " << address.get_printable();
```

Output
```
Target write community = private
Target read community = private
Target address = 15.29.33.210
```

CHAPTER 9

The Snmp Class

This chapter presents the SNMP++ Snmp class. The Snmp class ties together all of the classes within the SNMP++ framework to provide for interaction with SNMP managed agents. Described are the Snmp class and its member functions for SNMP versions 1 and 2 operations. In addition, the SnmpCollection class is presented, showing how collections of SNMP++ objects can be used to build advanced applications. See Figure 9.1 on the next page.

The most powerful class in SNMP++ is the Snmp class. The Snmp class is the encapsulation of an SNMP session where a session is a logical connection between a manager and one or more agents. SNMP++ provides a logical binding of a management application with an SNMP++ session to and from specified agents through the Snmp class. Handled by the Snmp Class are the construction, reliable delivery, and reception of Protocol Data Units (PDUs). Most Application Programmer Interfaces (APIs) require the programmer to directly manage this session. This includes providing reliability over unreliable transport mechanisms such as handling time-outs, retries, and duplication of SNMP PDUs. The Snmp class manages the session and frees the implementor to concentrate on the agent management. By going through the Snmp class for session management, the implementor is driving through well-developed and tested code. The alternative is to design, implement, and test your own SNMP session engine. The Snmp class manages a session by: a) managing the transport layer over the User Datagram Protocol (UDP) or Internetwork Packet Exchange (IPX) transports; b) handling the packaging and unpackaging of variable bindings into PDUs; c) providing for the delivery and reception of PDUs; and, d) managing all necessary memory and SNMP resources.

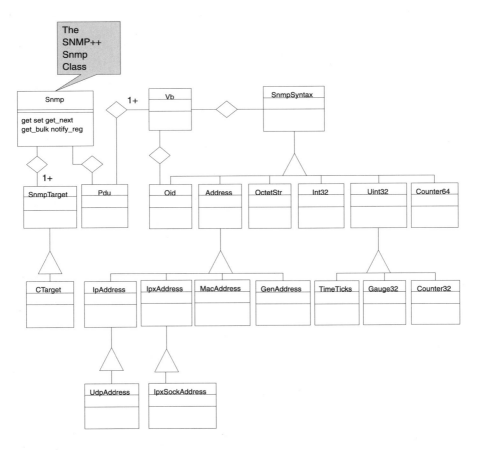

Figure 9.1 Object Modeling Technique (OMT) Object Model View of the Snmp Class.

The Snmp class is easy to use. Six basic member functions, `Snmp::get()`, `Snmp::set()`, `Snmp::get_next()`, `Snmp::get_bulk()`, `Snmp::inform()`, and `Snmp::trap()` provide the basic functions a network management application needs. Blocking or nonblocking (asynchronous) forms can be used. Notification sending and receiving are supported through the `Snmp::trap()` and `Snmp::inform()` member functions. Receiving notifications are supported through the `Snmp::notify_register()` and `Snmp::notify_unregister()` member functions.

The Snmp class is safe to use. The constructor and destructors allocate and de-allocate all memory and resources that are needed. This minimizes the likelihood of corrupt or leaking memory. All of the internal SNMP mechanisms are hidden and thus cannot be modified inadvertently. The Snmp class is portable. Its interface is portable across Operating Systems (OSs) and Network Operating Systems (NOSs).

BILINGUAL API

All Snmp class member functions are bilingual. That is, they can be used with identical parameter lists to access MIB information from SNMP version 1 or version 2 agents. This frees the programmer from having to modify code to deal with an SNMP version 2 agent. Once an SnmpTarget has been created, all Snmp class member functions behave the same way. The lower level internals of the SNMP++ determine whether or not the SnmpTarget is SNMP version 1 or version 2 and decide how to deal with the differences for you. From the perspective of the API, SNMP++ provides an SNMP version 2 view of the world. What this means is that an application developer can think of all agents from an SNMP version 2 perpective. One feature that makes this possible is that the *Get-Bulk* operation is mapped to *Get-Next* for SNMP version 1 agents.

SNMP CLASS CONSTRUCTORS AND DESTRUCTORS

The constructors and destructors for the Snmp class enable sessions to be opened and closed. When an Snmp object is constructed, an Snmp session is opened. UDP or IPX sockets are created and managed until the object is destroyed. Snmp objects can be instantiated dynamically or statically. See Table 9.1 on the next page.

Table 9.1   Snmp Class Constructor and Destructor.

Snmp Class Constructor and Destructor	Description
Constructor	
Snmp::Snmp(int &status);	Construct an Snmp object, status indicates success.
Destructor	
Snmp::~Snmp( );	Destructor, frees all resources, closes the session.

Snmp Class Constructor

A required construction parameter is return status. Since constructors do not return values in C++, the caller must provide a status that should be checked after the object is instantiated. The caller should check the return status for SNMP_CLASS_SUCCESS. (See Example 9.1.) If the construction status does not indicate success, the session should not be used. To further determine the actual error, the Snmp::error_msg() member function can be used.

Example 9.1   Construction of an Snmp Object.

```
int status;
Snmp snmp( status);                        // construct an Snmp object
if ( status != SNMP_CLASS_SUCCESS)
   cout << "Error Constructing Snmp Object! \n";
else
   cout << "Success Constructing Snmp Object \n";
```

Output
```
Success Constructing Snmp Object
```

Snmp Class Destructor

The Snmp class destructor closes the session and releases all resources and memory. (See Example 9.2.) Destruction is automatic for statically declared objects; this happens when the object goes out of scope. For a dynamically instantiated object, using C++'s *new* operator, destruction occurs when the C++ *delete* construct is used.

Example 9.2   Destruction of an Snmp Object.

```
int status;
Snmp *snmp;
snmp = new Snmp(status);              // construct an Snmp object
if (status != SNMP_CLASS_SUCCESS)
    cout << << "Error Constructing Snmp Object! \n";
.
.
delete snmp;                          // delete an Snmp object
```

SNMP CLASS PUBLIC MEMBER FUNCTIONS

The Snmp class provides a variety of member functions, as shown in Table 9.2 on the next page, to create, manage, and terminate a session. Multiple Snmp objects can be instantiated at the same time. The Snmp class supports member functions for performing SNMP Gets, Sets, Get-Nexts, and Get-Bulks. SNMP++ provides these functions in both a blocked and an asynchronous flavor.

Table 9.2   Snmp Class Access Member Functions.

Snmp Class Member Functions	Description
`int get( Pdu &pdu, SnmpTarget &target);`	Invokes blocked SNMP Get. Gets Pdu from target.
`int set( Pdu &pdu, SnmpTarget &target);`	Invokes blocked SNMP Set. Sets Pdu from target.
`int get_next( Pdu &pdu,` `        SnmpTarget &target);`	Invokes blocked SNMP Get-Next, using Pdu from target.

`int get_bulk( Pdu &pdu,`
`        SnmpTarget &target,`
`        const int non_repeaters,`
`        const int max_reps);`
	Invokes blocked SNMP Get-Bulk (V2 targets only otherwise uses Get-Next).

`int get( Pdu &pdu,`
`        SnmpTarget &target,`
`        snmp_callback callback,`
`        void * callback_data=0);`
	Invokes SNMP asynchronous Get. Gets Pdu from target, uses defined callback and callback data.

`int set( Pdu &pdu,`
`        SnmpTarget &target,`
`        snmp_callback callback,`
`        void * callback_data=0);`
	Invokes SNMP asynchronous Set. Sets Pdu from target, uses defined callback and callback data.

`int get_next( Pdu &pdu,`
`        SnmpTarget &target,`
`        snmp_callback callback,`
`        void * callback_data=0);`
	Invokes SNMP asynchronous Get-Next. Get-Next Pdu from target, uses defined callback and callback data.

`int get_bulk( Pdu &pdu,`
`        SnmpTarget &target,`
`        const int non_repeaters,`
`        const int max_reps`
`        snmp_callback callback,`
`        void * callback_data=0);`
	Invokes SNMP asynchronous Get-Bulk. Get-Bulk Pdu from target, uses defined callback and callback data. (V2 targets only otherwise uses Get-Next.)

Snmp Class Blocked Get Member Function

The `Snmp::get()` member function enables you to get objects from the agent at the specified target. The caller must specify the destination target and requested Pdu. This call blocks until either the response from the designated target is received or an error is encountered. Once a valid response is received, the response Pdu object can be used to extract the variable bindings that were processed by the target agent.

Example 9.3 performs an SNMP Get for the sysDescr object from the agent at IP address 10.4.8.5. If successful, the result is displayed.

Example 9.3   Snmp Class Blocked Get Member Function.

```
int status;
Snmp snmp( status);                    // construct an Snmp object
// check status for success on construction
if ( status != SNMP_CLASS_SUCCESS) {
   cout << snmp.error_msg( status);
   return;
}
Vb vb;                                 // create a vb object
vb.set_oid("1.3.6.1.2.1.1.1.0");       // load the Oid portion with
                                       // the variable id to get
Pdu pdu;                               // create a Pdu object
pdu += vb;                             // attach the vb to the pdu
CTarget target("10.4.8.5");            // create a target
// invoke the get…
if ((status = snmp.get( pdu, target)) == SNMP_CLASS_SUCCESS) {
   pdu.get_vb( vb,0);                  // extract the vb from the pdu
   cout << vb.get_printable_oid() << "=";
   cout << vb.get_printable_value();// print out the vb value
}
else
   cout << snmp.error_msg( status); // if there's an error, print it
```

Output
```
1.3.6.1.2.1.1.1.0 = NT Workstation Version 4.0
```

Snmp Class Blocked Get-Next Member Function

When invoking an SNMP Get, an exact instance of an MIB object is retrieved. The Get-Next operation, however, retrieves the next instance, or the instance that follows, the MIB object requested. SNMP++ provides both blocked and member functions for invoking a Get-Next.

Example 9.4 will walk the entire MIB for the agent found at
`10.4.8.5` and displays all the MIB objects. When the end of the MIB is
reached, an error will be returned and the while loop will terminate.

Example 9.4   Snmp Class Blocked Mode Get-Next Member Function.

```
int status;
Snmp snmp( status);                // construct an Snmp object
// check status for success on construction
if ( status != SNMP_CLASS_SUCCESS) {
   cout << snmp.error_msg( status);
   return;
}
Vb vb;                             // create a variable binding object
vb.set_oid("1");                   // start at the beginning of an MIB
Pdu pdu;                           // create a Pdu object
pdu += vb;                         // attach the vb to the Pdu
CTarget target("10.4.8.5");        // create a target
// while get-next succeeds, keep going
while ((status = snmp.get_next(pdu,target)))==SNMP_CLASS_SUCCESS) {
   pdu.get_vb( vb,0);              // extract the vb from the pdu
   cout << vb.get_printable_value() << "\n"; // print out the value
}
cout << snmp.error_msg( status);
```

Output
Entire contents of agent's MIB @ 10.4.8.5

Snmp Class Blocked Set Member Function

The Snmp class provides a member function to invoke the SNMP
Set operation. Unlike the Get or Get-Next operation, using the
`Snmp::set()` member function requires loading both the Oid portion
and value portion of each Vb object that is to be set in the Pdu object. The
example that follows assumes that the agent at IP address `10.4.8.5`
allows SNMP write access to the MIB object at `1.3.6.1.2.1.1.4.0`
with a community name of *public*.

Example 9.5 sets the sysContact MIB object on the agent at IP address 10.4.8.5 to the value Coho.

Example 9.5   Snmp Class Blocked Mode Set Member Function.

```
int status;
Snmp snmp( status);               // construct an Snmp object
// check status for success on construction
if ( status != SNMP_CLASS_SUCCESS) {
   cout << snmp.error_msg( status);
   return;
}
Vb vb;                            // create a vb object
vb.set_oid("1.3.6.1.2.1.1.4.0");  // set the Oid portion of the Vb
vb.set_value("Coho");             // set the value portion
Pdu pdu;                          //construct a Pdu
pdu += vb;                        // attach the Vb
CTarget target("10.4.8.5");       // create a target
// invoke a set…
status = snmp.set( pdu, target);
cout << snmp.error_msg( status);  // result of the operation
```

Output
SNMP++ Operation Successful

Snmp Class Blocked Get-Bulk Member Function

SNMP++ provides a Get-Bulk interface for working with both SNMP version 1 and version 2 agents. For SNMP version 1 operations, this member function maps over Get-Next. Get-Bulk vastly improves the efficiency of getting large amounts of data from an agent. Rather than traverse an agent's MIB via Get-Next, Get-Bulk enables the agent to Get-Next the data locally and transfer the result in bulk across the wire back to the manager. In order to provide a flexible bulk transfer mechanism, two additional parameters are included with the member function: the number of non-repeaters and the number of maximum repetitions.

Non-Repeaters The non-repeaters value represents variable bindings in the Pdu that should be retrieved once at most. This is beneficial when a manager requires a repeating variable binding in each Get-Bulk response from an agent. For example, a manager may want to retrieve a timestamp (sysUptime) along with table entries. The table entries may represent data that is accumulated rapidly; thus a timestamp on each response may be necessary. In this case, the first Vb object in the Pdu specifies sysUptime and the non-repeater value is one. This ensures that every Get-Bulk response has a sysUptime within it.

Max-Repetitions The maximum repetition value denotes the maximum number of times that the other variables, beyond the non-repeaters, should be retrieved. Essentially this defines the number of Get-Nexts that the agent should perform on each variable binding beyond the non-repeaters. One important feature of Get-Bulk is that it is a manager's responsibility to determine when to stop calling Get-Bulk. Get-Bulk may overrun the table being requested. It is the manager's responsibility to determine when this occurs and to ignore the extra Vbs. This is determined by examining the Get-Bulk response to see when the table requested was exhausted.

Example 9.6 performs a blocked mode Get-Bulk from the agent at IP address 10.4.8.5. This Get-Bulk example grabs up to ten Vbs per payload.

Example 9.6   Blocked Mode Get-Bulk Member Function.

```
int status;
Snmp snmp( status);
if ( status != SNMP_CLASS_SUCCESS) {
   cout << snmp.error_msg( status); return; }
Vb vb;
vb.set_oid("1");                    // refer to the start of the MIB
Pdu pdu;
pdu += vb;
CTarget target("10.4.8.5");
while ((status = snmp.get_bulk(pdu,target,0,10)))
              == SNMP_CLASS_SUCCESS) {
   int x = pdu.get_vb_count();
   for (int y=1;y<x;x++) {
```

```
        pdu.get_vb( vb,x);
        cout << vb.get_printable_oid() << "\n";
        cout << vb.get_printable_value << "\n";
    }
    pdu.trim(pdu.gett_vb_count()-1);  // Nuke all the Vbs
    pdu+=vb;                          // use last vb in next request
}
cout << snmp.error_msg( status);
```

Output
Entire contents of agent's MIB @ 10.4.8.5

SNMP CLASS ASYNCHRONOUS MEMBER FUNCTIONS

An Snmp class instance can support both blocked mode and asynchronous mode requests. Asynchronous requests return thread of control immediately and do not require that the caller wait for the response. The call returns when the request has been assembled and issued. The status indicates the success of sending the request. The response, however, is returned when the callback specified in the callback parameter is called. An additional parameter, the callback data parameter, is returned to the callback when it is called. This enables carrying additional user-specific information along with each request.

When to Use Blocked Mode vs. When to Use Asynchronous Mode

Given that two modes of operation are available, one must decide when one is more appropriate than the other. For programs in which event systems are present, such as Graphical User Interface (GUI) programs, asynchronous mode is the preferred choice. This is because blocked calls in an event system environment are blocking and will prevent other events from occurring. Asynchronous mode cooperates with the Operating System (OS) event system, allowing other events to happen as they need to. For non-GUI applications, such as text-mode console programs, an event system is not present and therefore blocked mode works fine.

SNMP++ Asynchronous Callback Function Type Definition

See Example 9.7 for the asynchronous callback function definition.

Example 9.7   Asynchronous Callback Definition.

```
typedef void (*snmp_callback)( int,     // reason callback is called
                               Snmp*,         // session handle
                               Pdu &,         // Pdu passed in
                               SnmpTarget &,  // source target
                               void * );      // callback data
```

Description of Reason Callback Parameter   The reason parameter is an integer that describes why the callback was called. The callback may have been called for a variety of reasons. A summary is described in Table 9.3.

Table 9.3   Asynchronous Mode Callback Reasons and Descriptions.

Callback Reason	Description
SNMP_CLASS_ASYNC_RESPONSE	An SNMP response has been received. This is a response to a Get, Set, Get-Next, Get-Bulk, or Inform. The Pdu parameter holds actual response PDU and the SnmpTarget parameter holds the target that issued the response.
SNMP_CLASS_TIMEOUT	An SNMP++ request has timed-out based on the time-out and retry information provided in the target instance. The Pdu parameter holds the original request Pdu for reuse. The SnmpTarget parameter holds the original target.
SNMP_CLASS_SESSION_DESTROYED	The session has been destroyed. All pending asynchronous requests were not completed.

SNMP_CLASS_NOTIFICATION

A notification, trap, or inform request has arrived. The Pdu object holds the actual notify. The notification ID, timestamp, and enterprise are available through Pdu member functions `Pdu::get_notify_id()`, `Pdu::get_notify_timestamp()`, and `Pdu::get_notifty_enterprise()`.

Description of Snmp++ Session Parameter This parameter holds the value of the session that made the request. This allows the session to be reused in time-out or Get-Next condition.

Description of Response PDU Parameter This parameter holds the response Pdu for responses, notifies, and traps. If the reason was a failure, the Pdu parameter holds the original request Pdu.

Description of Target Parameter This parameter holds the source of the Pdu for responses, notifies, and traps. If the reason was a failure, the value is the original target that was used when the request was made.

Description of Callback Data Parameter An optional argument can be provided enabling callback data when the request is placed. This information is returned in this parameter if it was specified. If it was not specified, this value is null.

Snmp Class Asynchronous Get Member Function

Like the blocked mode `Snmp::get()` member function, the asynchronous form performs an SNMP Get using a Pdu and SnmpTarget object. (See Example 9.8 on the next page.) Unlike the blocked mode form, the asynchronous form returns control to the caller once the request has been issued to the agent. The defined callback is called when the response PDU has arrived. The implementation of the caller's callback may utilize the response payload in any desired manner.

Example 9.8   Asynchronous Get.

```
// callback to be used for reception of responses
void my_callback( int reason,           // why callback is called
                  Snmp * session,       // session used to issue request
                  Pdu &pdu,             // Pdu object, content based on
                                        // reason
                  SnmpTarget &target,   // Target object, content based
                                        // on reason
                  void * callback_data) // optional user specified
                                        // callback data
{
   if ( reason == SNMP_CLASS_ASYNC_RESPONSE) {
      Vb vb;
      pdu.get_vb( vb,0);
      cout << vb.get_printable_oid() <<   " = " <<
      vb.get_printable_value() << "\n";
      }
      else
        cout << snmp->error_msg( reason) << "\n";
};

int status;
Snmp snmp( status);
if ( status != SNMP_CLASS_SUCCESS) {
   cout << snmp.error_msg( status); return; }
Vb vb;
vb.set_oid("1.3.6.1.2.1.1.1.0");
Pdu pdu;
pdu += vb;
CTarget target("10.4.8.5");
if ((status = snmp.get( pdu, target,my_callback,0)) !
           = SNMP_CLASS_SUCCESS)
     cout << snmp.error_msg( status);
```

Output
```
1.3.6.1.2.1.1.1.0 = NT Workstation Version 4.0
```

Snmp Class Asynchronous Get-Next Member Function

The asynchronous Snmp::get_next() member function works in the same way as the other asynchronous member functions. It requires a callback function and an optional callback data parameter. Rather than return the MIB object instance specified, Get-Next returns the next instance in the MIB for all variables requested. See Example 9.9.

Example 9.9   Asynchronous Get-Next.

```
// callback to be used for reception of responses
void my_callback( int reason,          // why callback is called
                  Snmp * session,      // session used to issue request
                  Pdu &pdu,            // Pdu object, content based on
                                       // reason
                  SnmpTarget &target,  // Target object, content based
                                       // on reason
                  void * callback_data)  // optional user specified
                                         // callback data
{
    if ( reason == SNMP_CLASS_ASYNC_RESPONSE)   {
      Vb vb;
       pdu.get_vb( vb,0);
       cout << vb.get_printable_oid() << " = " <<
       vb.get_printable_value() << "\n";
       // call get-next again with response Pdu
       snmp->get_next( pdu,target, my_callback0);
    }
    else
       cout << snmp->error_msg( reason) << "\n";
};

int status;
Snmp snmp( status);
if ( status != SNMP_CLASS_SUCCESS) {
   cout << snmp.error_msg( status); return; }
Vb vb;
vb.set_oid("1");
Pdu pdu;
pdu += vb;
CTarget target("10.4.8.5");
// first get-next request starts process, callback takes over from here
if ((status = snmp.get_next( pdu, target,my_callback,0)) !
            = SNMP_CLASS_SUCCESS)
     cout << snmp.error_msg( status);
```

Output
Entire contents of agent's MIB @ 10.4.8.5

Snmp Class Asynchronous Set Member Function

The asynchronous Snmp::set() member function works in the same manner as the blocked mode request except that it requires a callback function and an optional callback data parameter. See Example 9.10.

Example 9.10   Asynchronous Set.

```
// callback to be used for reception of responses
void my_callback( int reason,           // why callback is called
                  Snmp * session,       // session used to issue request
                  Pdu &pdu,             // Pdu content based on reason
                  SnmpTarget &target,   // Target object, content based
                                        // on reason
                  void * callback_data) // optional user specified
                                        // callback data
{
    if ( reason == SNMP_CLASS_ASYNC_RESPONSE)
        cout << "Asynchronous Set Successful \n";
    else
        cout << snmp->error_msg( reason) << "\n";
};

int status;
Snmp snmp( status);
if ( status != SNMP_CLASS_SUCCESS) {
    cout << snmp.error_msg( status); return; }
Vb vb;
vb.set_oid("1.3.6.1.2.1.1.3.0");
vb.set_value("Level 42");
Pdu pdu;
pdu += vb;
CTarget target("10.4.8.5");
if ((status = snmp.set( pdu,target, my_callback,0)) !
            = SNMP_CLASS_SUCCESS)
        cout << snmp.error_msg( status);
```

Output
```
Asynchronous Set Successful
```

Snmp Class Asynchronous Get-Bulk Member Function

Like the blocked form, the asynchronous form of Get-Bulk requires a non-repeaters and maximum repetition value. For this Get-Bulk example, the number of max-repeaters used is zero, which indicates no repeating Vbs with each response. See Example 9.11.

Example 9.11 Asynchronous Get-Bulk.

```
// callback to be used for reception of responses
void my_callback( int reason,        // why callback is called
                  Snmp * session,    // session used to issue request
                  Pdu &pdu,          // Pdu content based on reason
                  SnmpTarget &target, // Target object, content based
                                     // on reason
                  void * callback_data) // optional user specified
                                     // callback data
{
    if ( reason == SNMP_CLASS_ASYNC_RESPONSE)  {
      Vb vb;
      int x = pdu.get_vb_count();
      while ( int y=0; y<x; x++) {
         pdu.get_vb( vb,x);
         cout << vb.get_printable_oid() << " = " <<
         vb.get_printable_value() << "\n"; }
      pdu.trim( x-1);
      pdu.set_vb( vb,0);                    // adjust for next get-bulk
       // call get-bulk again with response Pdu
       snmp->get_bulk( pdu,target, 0,1,my_callback0);
    }
    else
       cout << snmp->error_msg( reason) << "\n";
};

int status;
Snmp snmp( status);
if ( status != SNMP_CLASS_SUCCESS) {
   cout << snmp.error_msg( status); return; }
Vb vb;
vb.set_oid("1");
Pdu pdu;
pdu += vb;
CTarget target("10.4.8.5");
// first get-bulk request starts process, callback takes over from here
if ((status = snmp.get_bulk( pdu, target,0,1,my_callback,0)) !
            = SNMP_CLASS_SUCCESS)
     cout << snmp.error_msg( status);
```
Output
Entire contents of agent's MIB @ 10.4.8.5

Canceling an Asynchronous Request

SNMP++ allows asynchronous requests to be canceled before they have been completed. This is useful for situations when your code may need to exit prematurely or when the specified callback is no longer available. Asynchronous requests are canceled automatically when the Snmp object used to issue the requests is destroyed. When this happens, the specified callback receives a SNMP_CLASS_SESSION_DESTROYED reason. Alternatively, an individual asynchronous request can be canceled using the Snmp::cancel() member function. This member function silently cancels the asynchronous request specified with the request ID parameter.

Table 9.4   Asynchronous Cancel Member Function.

Snmp Class Member Functions	Description
int cancel(const unsigned long rid);	Cancels an asynchronous request.

Once an asynchronous request is issued, the caller can extract the request identifier from the Pdu object. This request ID can be used to cancel a particular request. (See Example 9.12.) Again, this is required only where the Snmp object that issued the request is still active.

Example 9.12   Canceling an Asynchronous Request.

```
Snmp->cancel(  request_id);
```

SNMP++ NOTIFICATION METHODS

The SNMP++ API supports member functions for both sending and receiving notifications. In SNMP version 2 terminology, traps are commonly referred to as notifications and throughout this book traps and notifications may be used interchangeably.

Table 9.5   Snmp Class Notification Member Functions.

Snmp Class Notification Member Functions	Description

`int inform( Pdu &pdu,`
`         SnmpTarget &target,`
`         snmp_callback callback,`
`         void * callback_data=0);`
	Invokes asynchronous inform. Uses notify callback.

`int inform( Pdu &pdu,` `         SnmpTarget &target);`	Blocked Inform member function.
`int trap( Pdu &pdu,` `        SnmpTarget &target);`	Sends a trap to the specified target.

`int notify_register( TargetCollection &targets,`
`                 OidCollection &trapids,`
`                 snmp_callback callback,`
`                 void * callback_data=0);`
	Register to receive traps and/or informs.

`int notify_register( TargetCollection &targets,`
`                 OidCollection &trapids,`
`                 AddressCollection`
`                 &listen_addresses,`
`                 snmp_callback callback,`
`                 void * callback_data=0);`
	Register to receive traps and/or informs and specify listen interfaces using the AddressCollection.

`int notify_unregister();`	Unregister to receive traps and/or informs.

Sending Traps

Sending traps is a useful part of a manager API that allows notifications to be passed to other management stations. This can be useful in domain management where a network management station is used to manage a local domain of managed agents. When a certain condition arises, this station may send a notification to a manager of manager station.

Send Trap Member Function Parameter Descriptions

Pdu &pdu   The Pdu to send. This is where the payload of the trap is contained. The payload of a trap is comprised of a Pdu object, and its Variable Binding contents are dependent on the vendor-specific information to be sent.

SnmpTarget &target   In this role, the SnmpTarget denotes where
to send the trap.

Specifying the ID of a Trap   Trap IDs are specified in the same
way as Inform Ids. Using the `Pdu::set_notify_id()` member function, the ID of a trap PDU can be specified. Trap identifiers are represented using the SNMP version 2 trap identifiers, which are represented using Oids. To create a trap ID, simply create an Oid object
with the desired trap ID value, then attach it to a Pdu using the
`Pdu::set_notify_id()` member function. Conversely, the ID of a trap
can be obtained using the `Pdu::get_notify_id()` member function.

IETF Oids for Generic Traps   To send an enterprise-specific trap,
the caller can specify an Oid that is not in the generic set specified in
Table 9.6.

Table 9.6   Oid for Generic Traps.

Trap Type	Trap Oid
coldStart	`1.3.6.1.6.3.1.1.5.1`
warmStart	`1.3.6.1.6.3.1.1.5.2`
linkDown	`1.3.6.1.6.3.1.1.5.3`
linkUp	`1.3.6.1.6.3.1.1.5.4`
authenticationFailure	`1.3.6.1.6.3.1.1.5.5`
egpNeighborLoss	`1.3.6.1.6.3.1.1.5.6`

Specifying the TimeStamp on a Trap   To specify the timestamp on
a trap PDU, the `Pdu::set_notify_timestamp()` member function can
be used. If a Pdu is sent without calling this member function, a timestamp from the SNMP++ engine is utilized.

Specifying the Trap Enterprise   Not to be confused with enterprise-specific traps, the enterprise of any trap represents the origin of the trap in an agent's MIB. Typically, this is the System Object Identifier of the trap sender, but in theory it can take on any Oid value. In order to accommodate this parameter, SNMP++ allows setting the enterprise using the `Pdu::set_notify_enterprise()` member function. This is an optional call. If used, the enterprise provided is attached to the Pdu object.

Specifying Specific Trap Values for SNMP Version 1 Traps   To specify an SNMP version 1–specific value, the trapid Oid should be constructed as follows. The last subid of the trapid represents the specific value to use. The second to the last subid should be zero. So, to specify a trap-specific value, two extra subids must be appended, a zero and a value or "0.X." This convention is consistent with RFC 1908, which specifies SNMP version 1 to SNMP version 2 trap mappings. See Example 9.13.

Example 9.13   Sending a Trap.

```
void send_trap()
{
    int status;                               // return status
    CTarget target( (IpAddress) "10.4.8.5");  // SNMP++ v1 target
    Pdu pdu;                                  // SNMP++ PDU

    //——-[ Construct an SNMP++ SNMP Object ]————-
    Snmp snmp( status);                       // Create an SNMP++ session
    if ( status != SNMP_CLASS_SUCCESS) {      // check creation status
        cout << snmp.error_msg(status); // if fail, print error string
        return;   }
    pdu.set_notify_id( coldStart);
    status = snmp.trap( pdu, target);
    cout << " Trap Send Status = " << snmp.error_msg( status);
};
```

Inform Member Functions

Informs are available only in SNMP version 2. The inform is an acknowledged form of a notification. Traps are unacknowledged or trap PDUs generate no response PDU. Since traps are unacknowledged, a management entity that generates a trap has no way of knowing if the trap reached its desired destination. For notifications that are quite important, the inform operation offers the option of requiring a response. SNMP++ provides two member functions for informs, including a blocked and asynchronous form.

Snmp Class Asynchronous Inform Member Function

The asynchronous form of the inform operates in the same manner as all of the other SNMP++ asynchronous member functions. The call returns immediately after the inform request is issued. The inform response is called asynchronously to the callback when the response is received. The callback reason is SNMP_CLASS_ASYNC_RESPONSE, the inform response can be found in the Pdu payload.

Snmp Class Blocked Inform Member Function

In addition to the asynchronous form of the inform operation, SNMP++ provides a blocked form in which the response PDU is returned directly.

Specifying the ID of an Inform   Inform IDs are specified in the same manner as trap IDs. Using the Pdu::set_notify_id() member function, the ID of an inform PDU can be specified. Inform identifiers are represented using Oids. To create an Inform ID, simply create an Oid object with the desired inform ID value, then attach it to a Pdu using the Pdu::set_notify_id() member function. Conversely, the ID of a inform can be obtained using the Pdu::get_notify_id() member function.

Specifying the Timestamp on an Inform   To specify an inform timestamp, the Pdu::set_notify_timestamp() member function can be used. If a Pdu is sent without calling this member function, a timestamp from the SNMP++ engine is utilized.

Receiving Notifications

SNMP++ trap and inform reception enable applications to receive traps and informs based on caller-specified filtering. Unlike other SNMP operations, informs and traps are unsolicited events that can occur at any time. Informs and traps, therefore, are asynchronous events. SNMP++ provides member functions that enable caller-specified filtering of informs and traps. Informs and traps can be filtered based on their type, source, and destination.

Trap and Inform Registration and the Snmp Class

Each Snmp class instance can be registered for its own unique set of traps or informs. That is, an Snmp object can have its own set of filters and a callback to invoke when a trap or inform arrives meeting the filter criteria. The `Snmp::notify_register()` member function can be invoked multiple times when each new call clears the previous filter settings. Trap and inform reception for a particular session ceases when either the `Snmp::notify_unregister()` member function is invoked or when the Snmp instance is destroyed.

`Snmp::notify_register()`, Basic Form

The basic or typical form for notification registration includes notification type and notification source filtering parameters, or an OidCollection and a TargetCollection. Using this form of `notify_register()` causes notification listening to occur on all local interfaces. Thus, if the local machine is multi-homed (it has multiple network interfaces), all interfaces are opened up for notify reception using the well-known port/socket numbers. For example, say my machine has two network cards, both running the Internet Protocol (IP) and only one using the Internet Exchange Protocol (IPX). Calling the basic form of `notify_register()` listens on both IP interfaces using the well-known SNMP trap port, and on the IPX interface using the well-known trap IPX socket number.

`Snmp::notify_register()`, Alternate Form

The alternate or name-overloaded form of `notify_register()` accepts one additional parameter that enables specification of the local interface to listen for notifications, or the AddressCollection. The AddressCollection parameter contains a list of Address objects to listen to, including IpAddresses, IpxAddresses, UdpAddresses, and IpxSockAddresses. A list of interpretations of Addresses in the Collection and how `notify_register()` will behave follows in Table 9.7 on the next page.

AddressCollection Element Behavior Definition

The `Snmp::notify_register()` member function requires a collection of addresses to denote the desired filtering. The collection represents an ordered collection of Address objects. SNMP++ provides a collection class to collect SNMP++ objects, including Addresses. When used with the `Snmp::notify_register()` member function, the individual elements of the collection have specific meaning. They are defined in Table 9.7.

Table 9.7   Notification Reception Filtering Behavior.

Address Class	Value	Description
IpAddress	Any value except `0.0.0.0`	Listen on IP interface specified using well-known IP port.
IpAddress	`0.0.0.0`	Listen on all IP interfaces using well-known IP port.
UdpAddress	Any value except `0.0.0.0`	Listen on IP interface specified using IP port specified.
UdpAddress	`0.0.0.0`	Listen on all IP interfaces using IP port specified.
IpxAddress	Any value except `00000000:000000000000`	Listen on IPX interface specified using well-known IPX socket number.
IpxAddress	`00000000:000000000000`	Listen on all IPX interfaces using well-known IPX socket number.
IpxSockAddress	Any value except `00000000:000000000000`	Listen on IPX interface specified using socket number specified.
IpxSockAddress	`00000000:000000000000`	Listen on all IPX interfaces using socket number specified.

Filter Behavior of `notify_regsiter()`   When active, filters behave as follows. If an incoming inform or trap matches any item in the OidCollection of IDs **AND** the incoming inform or trap matches any item in the TargetCollection **THEN** the inform/trap is forwarded to the caller's specified callback. Note, if the OidCollection is empty then all informs will pass the ID check. If the TargetCollection is empty, then all informs will pass the Target check.

Filtering Using OidCollection, TargetCollection, and AddressCollections

SNMP++ provides three ordered collection classes for putting together collections of Oids, Targets, and Addresses. All collection classes operate in an identical manner because they are derived from the same C++ Template, SnmpCollection. For more information on the SnmpCollection class, please refer to the section on SnmpCollections.

SNMP++ CLASS ERROR RETURN CODES

There are a variety of return codes provided for use with SNMP++. The error codes are common across platforms and can aid the application programmer in finding and detecting error conditions their application.

Snmp Class Error Message Member Function

If an error occurs during use of the Snmp member function, the Snmp::error_msg() member function (see Table 9.8) can be used to retrieve a user-friendly error string. See Example 9.14 for a demonstration on how to print an SNMP++ error message.

Table 9.8   Snmp Error Message.

SNMP++ Error Message	Description
char * Snmp::error_msg(const int status);	Returns a string based on the value passed in.

Example 9.14   Printing an SNMP++ Error Message.

```
int status;
Snmp snmp( status);
cout << snmp.error_msg( status);
```

Output
```
SNMP++: Success
```

OPERATIONAL MODES

SNMP++ is designed to support a variety of operational modes. The modes of operation enable the construction of Graphical User Interface (GUI) and console-mode applications. GUI operational mode cooperates with the existing GUI event systems while console mode operational mode allows for utilization of a custom event system or no event system at all.

Microsoft Windows Event System Operation

For MS-Windows usage, SNMP++ cooperates with the MS-Windows messaging system. Blocked mode calls enable other messages to be processed. Although this works, asynchronous mode is advocated for MS-Windows development.

Open Systems Foundation (OSF) X11 Motif Operation

The X11 interface is identical to the MS-Windows interface. Both MS-Windows and X11 versions of SNMP++ support blocked and asynchronous modes of usage. One additional function call is required for an X11 application to register its X11 context with SNMP++ so that SNMP++ can take advantage of X11's event system. (See Table 9.9.) This enables `XtAppMainLoop()` or similar functions to recognize and dispatch all asynchronous SNMP++ events transparently.

- The context parameter passed in is returned from a call to `XtAppInitialize()`.
- The return value is zero if the function is successful in registering with X11.

Table 9.9   X11 Initialization.

X11 Motif Operation Function	Description
`int SNMPX11Initialize( XtAppContext context);`	Allows adding X11 context to SNMP++ event system.

Non-GUI-Based Application Operation

A third operational mode for SNMP++ is the use for constructing text-mode console applications. Such applications can operate using either blocked-mode or asynchronous-mode calls. For blocked-mode calls, no additional SNMP++ function calls are needed. Asynchronous calls require use of some event system. For console operational asynchronous mode, SNMP++ offers a set of function calls to read the currently used file descriptors (socket handles) that the caller can then utilize in their own 'select' call. If an SNMP++ file descriptor has a pending event, the caller can invoke a routine to process all pending events.

SNMPGetFdSets   SNMPGetFdSets is used to determine which file descriptors potentially will be active. The function fills in read, write, and exception masks which then can be passed to "select." See Table 9.10.

Table 9.10   UNIX Obtaining Current File Descriptors.

X11 Motif Operation Function	Description

`int SNMPGetFdSets( int &maxfds,`
`                    fd_set &read_fds,`
`                    fd_set &write_fds,`
`                    fd_set &exceptfds);`
	Enables the current set of file descriptors in use to be obtained.

SNMPGetNextTimeout   SNMPGetNextTimeout is used to determine the time at which the next time-out event will occur. (See Table 9.11.) This value then can be used to determine the maximum interval that a blocked operation, such as select, should wait before returning control. The time-out calculation is based on the closest time of all user-registered time-outs and SNMP retransmission time-outs.

Table 9.11   UNIX Getting the Next Time-Out Period.

X11 Motif Operation Function	Description
`unsigned long int SNMPGetNextTimeout( );`	Get the next time-out period. Returned in 1/100 of a second.

SNMPProcessPendingEvents SNMPProcessPendingEvents is used to process all currently outstanding events. (See Table 9.12.) This function can call any callbacks associated with completed time-outs, file descriptors, or outstanding SNMP messages. This function does not block; it handles only events outstanding at the time.

Table 9.12   UNIX Processing Pending Events.

X11 Motif Operation Function	Description
int SNMPProcessPendingEvents();	Process all pending events.

SNMP++ STATUS AND ERROR CODES

SNMP++ provides two error levels when it performs Snmp class operations. All Snmp class member functions return a status value. (See Table 9.13.) One special error value, SNMP_CLASS_ERR_STATUS_SET indicates that the Pdu has an internal error that must be retrieved via the Pdu::get_error_status() member function. All SNMP++ error values can be passed into the Snmp::error_msg() member function for a textual description of the error.

Table 9.13   Snmp Error Values.

SNMP++ General Errors	Value	Description
SNMP_CLASS_SUCCESS	0	Success Status.
SNMP_CLASS_ERROR	-1	General Error.
SNMP_CLASS_RESOURCE_UNAVAIL	-2	New or malloc Failed.
SNMP_CLASS_INTERNAL_ERROR	-3	Unexpected internal error.
SNMP_CLASS_UNSUPPORTED	-4	Unsupported function.
Callback Reasons		
SNMP_CLASS_TIMEOUT	-5	Outstanding request timed out.
SNMP_CLASS_ASYNC_RESPONSE	-6	Received response.
SNMP_CLASS_NOTIFICATION	-7	Received notification (trap/inform).
SNMP_CLASS_SESSION_DESTROYED	-8	Snmp Object destroyed.

Snmp Class Errors

SNMP_CLASS_INVALID	-10	Snmp member function called on invalid instance.
SNMP_CLASS_INVALID_PDU	-11	Invalid Pdu passed to mf.
SNMP_CLASS_INVALID_TARGET	-12	Invalid target passed to mf.
SNMP_CLASS_INVALID_CALLBACK	-13	Invalid callback to mf.
SNMP_CLASS_INVALID_REQID	-14	Invalid request ID to cancel.
SNMP_CLASS_INVALID_NOTIFYID	-15	Missing trap/inform Oid.
SNMP_CLASS_INVALID_OPERATION	-16	Snmp operation not allowed for specified target.
SNMP_CLASS_INVALID_OID	-17	Invalid Oid passed to mf.
SNMP_CLASS_INVALID_ADDRESS	-18	Invalid address passed to mf.
SNMP_CLASS_ERR_STATUS_SET	-19	Agent returned response Pdu with error status set.
SNMP_CLASS_TL_UNSUPPORTED	-20	Transport not supported.
SNMP_CLASS_TL_IN_USE	-21	Transport in use.
SNMP_CLASS_TL_FAILED	-22	Transport Failed.

SNMPCOLLECTIONS

Collections are an important part of object-oriented programming. Collections enable the collection of objects into groups, and in so doing simplify many tasks. SNMP++ includes a collection class, SnmpCollection, that enables collecting like objects in an unordered manner. The SnmpCollection class can be used to collect any objects, although it is used in SNMP++ to collect Snmp-related objects such as Addresses and Oids.

The basic SnmpCollection class is implemented using C++ Templates. The C++ template enables easy reuse of the SnmpCollection code without having to write a new class for each type of collection. The SnmpCollection class enables the construction, addition, finding, and iteration of elements within a collection. See Table 9.14 on the next page.

Table 9.14   SnmpCollection Class Member Functions.

Collection Class Member Functions	Description
Constructors	
`SnmpCollection::SnmpCollection(void);`	Construct an empty collection.
`SnmpCollection::SnmpCollection(const T &t);`	Construct a collection using a single element.
`SnmpCollection::SnmpCollection(const SnmpCollection<T> &c);`	Make a collection with another collection.
Destructor	
`SnmpCollection::~SnmpCollection();`	Destroy the collection, free up all resources.
Member Functions	
`int size();`	Return the size of the collection (how many elements there are).
`SnmpCollection & operator += ( T &t);`	Append an element to a collection.
`SnmpCollection & operator = ( SnmpCollection &collection);`	Assign a collection to another collection.
`T& operator[ ]( int p);`	Access an element in a collection.
`int set_element( const T& i, const int p);`	Set an existing element in a collection.
`int get_element( T& i, const int p);`	Get an element from a collection.
`apply( void f( T&))`	Iterate a function to all elements in the collection that accepts a single element as the parameter.
`int find( const T& i)`	Look for an element within the collection, return TRUE if found.

Special Features

The SnmpCollection class supports a member function to iterate a user-specified function serially across all elements in a collection. The `SnmpCollection::apply()` member function enables a caller to specify a function that accepts an element as a parameter. When iterated, the function is called n times, once for each element in the collection. The iterator member function is a powerful, easy way to access all elements within a collection.

Examples of Collections in SNMP++

The SNMP++ set of classes utilizes the SnmpCollection class for three types of collections. The AddressCollection, TargetCollection, and OidCollection enable the collection of Addresses, Targets, and Oids. See Example 9.15.

Example 9.15   Address Collection.

```
// iterator which prints out an address
void my_iterator( Address & a)
{
   cout << a.get_printable() << "\n";
};

AddressCollection my_addresses;
IpAddress ipa;
ipa = "10.4.8.5";
my_addresses += ipa;
ipa = "255.248.0.0";
my_addresses += ipa;
IpxAddress ipx;
ipx += "01020304-010203040506";

my_address.apply( my_iterator);
```

Output
```
10.4.8.5
255.248.0
01020304-010203040506
```

Part III:
Developing Network
Management Applications

Parts I and II of this book focus on network management, SNMP, and the details of SNMP++. This section focuses on putting all of the pieces together to construct real management applications using SNMP++. SNMP++ is a technology that has been used successfully in a variety of network management applications. Thus, SNMP++ has evolved to meet the needs of a broad range of applications, including Graphical User Interface (GUI)-based applications, text-mode console-based applications, and applications that integrate with network managment platforms such as Hewlett-Packard OpenView. In addition to using the SNMP protocol to manage agents, a management application requires many other important components that need to integrate with the overall management solution well. Next to SNMP, the most important of these may be the user interface. User interface considerations often drive the overall architecture of an application. A good Application Programmers Interface (API), therefore, should integrate well with common user interface systems such as windowing event systems. As will be illustrated in the chapters that follow, SNMP++ provides a number of special features that enable seamless integration with GUI systems.

CHAPTER 10

Writing Applications with SNMP++

S NMP++ is a C++ based Application Programmers Interface (API) that can be implemented to operate on any Operating System (OS) that supports an ANSI/ISO C++ compiler and network services over a standardized protocol for SNMP, such as IP or IPX. Presented in this chapter are two such implementations, one for the Microsoft Windows 32-bit (MS-Windows NT and MS-Windows 95) environment and another for Hewlett-Packard UNIX (HPUX). Both of these implementations, including full source code, can be found on the enclosed CD-ROM. The focus of this section is on examples for the MS-Windows 32-bit environment. A complete SNMP browser implementation is presented here, including using a 32-bit SNMP++ Dynamic Link Library (DLL).

SNMP++ FOR MICROSOFT WINDOWS 32-BIT ENVIRONMENTS

An SNMP++ DLL for usage with Microsoft 32-bit Windows applications is included on the accompanying CD-ROM. The DLL is constructed as a Microsoft Foundation Class (MFC) extension DLL. This enables application construction with the Microsoft Visual C++ (MSVC++) environment.

SNMP++ for Win32 relies on a standardized Windows SNMP API, WinSNMP, for the encoding and decoding of SNMP Abstract Syntax Notation One (ASN.1)/Basic Encoding Rules (BER) information. For operation on Win32, a WinSNMP DLL, therefore, is required. A copy of WinSNMP is also included on the CD-ROM.

WinSNMP and SNMP++

SNMP++ for Win32 requires a 32-bit WinSNMP Dynamic Link Library (DLL) for operation. This DLL must be present on the system where the SNMP++-based application is to reside. WinSNMP is a C-based SNMP API for the development of applications for the MS-Windows environment [WinSNMP]. Although effective, using a C-based API has many drawbacks, especially considering that most development on Win32 these days is accomplished using Microsoft Foundation Classes (MFC), which are C++ based. By having SNMP++ use WinSNMP there are benefits. One of these is the sharing of the well-known TCP/IP port (port 162) for SNMP trap reception. For SNMP standard trap reception, a single IP port number or IPX socket number must be used. Since there is only one port or socket, a single application owns it. For more than one application to receive traps and notifications, the trap port/socket must therefore be shared or multiplexed. WinSNMP provides this multiplexing and enables multiple SNMP++ applications to receive traps and notifications simultaneously. SNMP++ is designed to operate over any standard WinSNMP DLL and has been tested to operate with the most popular of these. In the near future, it is reasonable to expect that WinSNMP will become part of the MS-Win32 operating system much the same as happened with Windows Sockets [WinSock].

SNMP++ FOR HEWLETT-PACKARD UNIX (HPUX) ENVIRONMENTS

For the HPUX environment, SNMP++ utilizes its own ASN.1/BER encoding and decoding engine. SNMP++ for HPUX is bundled into a UNIX shared library. The complete source and make files for SNMP++ for HPUX are included on the CD-ROM that accompanies this book. Also included with the HPUX code are a number of examples, including X-Windows and text-mode examples.

DESCRIPTION OF HEADER FILES

In order to use SNMP++ within an application, a number of header files are required. (See Table 10.1.) An application need only include a single header file, snmp_pp.h, for operation. Below is a table and list of public header files used with SNMP++. These header files are common across Win32 or UNIX.

Table 10.1   SNMP++ Header Files.

SNMP++ Header File Name	Description
address.h	Definitions for Address classes, including IpAddress, IpxAddress, MacAddress, and GenAddress.
asn1.h	ASN.1 encoding and decoding function declarations.
collect.h	Definitions for SnmpCollection Template.
counter.h	Definition for Counter32 class.
ctr64.h	Definition for Counter64 class.
gauge.h	Definition for Gauge32 class.
integer.h	Definition for ASN.1 32-bit integer classes.
octet.h	Definition for OctetStr class.
oid.h	Definition for Oid class.
pdu.h	Definition for Pdu class.
smi.h	Definition of various SMI values and structures.
smival.h	Definition of SnmpSyntax class.
snmp_pp.h	Main header file for SNMP++. Only application developers need to include this file.
snmperrs.h	SNMP++ error messages and macros.
snmpmsg.h	SNMP++ SnmpMsg class, used for ASN.1 encoding of SNMP messages.
target.h	Definition of SnmpTarget and CTarget class.
timeticks.h	Definition of TimeTicks class.
vb.h	Definition of Variable Binding (Vb) class.

COMPACT DISC (CD-ROM) CONTENTS

A compact disc (CD-ROM) that contains a variety of useful information, source code, and examples accompanies this book. Included is the full SNMP++ source code for Win32 and HPUX. The source code enables you to build and use the SNMP++ libraries. In addition, a variety of example applications are included that can be used as is or inspected and modified to suite your needs. In addition to the SNMP++ code and examples, a variety of important documents are provided. These include the latest Internet Engineering Task Force (IETF) Request For Comments (RFCs) on the SNMP standard, a copy of the SNMP++ Open Specification Document, and a copy of the WinSNMP document.

SNMP++ Source Code

The source code for SNMP++ is provided for Win32 and HPUX. If you are not interested in the source, you can use the pre-built libraries directly. See Table 10.2.

Table 10.2   SNMP++ Source Code on CD-ROM.

CD-ROM Directories and Files	Description
Source Code	
snmp++\source\win32	Run SETUP.EXE from within this directory to install a Microsoft Visual C++ (MSVC++) project and SNMP++ source code for Win32. The setup program will step you through the installation. In addition to the source for building the SNMP++ DLL, the source for building a variety of text-mode example applications are provided.
snmp++\source\hpux	Within this directory can be found a UNIX tar file, snmp++.tar. Copy this file to the desired location on your HPUX machine and un-tar. Within the tar bundle can be found a readme.txt file that describes the contents in more detail.

SNMP++ Source Code Disclaimer SNMP++ is an open specification. Anyone is free to implement a version of SNMP++. Included with this text are implementations for Win32 and HPUX. Anyone is free to utilize the code provided they accept the following terms.

ATTENTION: USE OF THIS SOFTWARE IS
SUBJECT TO THE FOLLOWING TERMS.

Permission to use, copy, modify, distribute and/or sell this software and/or its documentation is hereby granted without fee. User agrees to display the above copyright notice and this license notice in all copies of the software and any documentation of the software. User agrees to assume all liability for the use of the software; Hewlett-Packard makes no representations about the suitability of this software for any purpose. It is provided "AS-IS" without warranty of any kind, either express or implied. User hereby grants a royalty-free license to any and all derivatives based upon this software code base.

SNMP++ Binaries and Header Files

For those who would like to use pre-built SNMP++ libraries, they can be copied directly from the CD-ROM without having to build them. Included are the header files, release, and debug build versions. See Table 10.3.

Table 10.3   SNMP++ Binaries on CD-ROM.

CD-ROM Directories and Files	Description
Binaries and Headers Win32	
snmp++\binaries\win32	Within this directory can be found two additional directories, one for release and another for debug.
snmp++\binaries\win32\release\snmp_pp.dll	Release build of SNMP++ for Win32. MFC extension DLL.

(continued)

Table 10.3 *(continued)*

CD-ROM Directories and Files	Description
`snmp++\binaries\win32\debug\snmp_pp.dll`	Debug build of SNMP++ for Win32. MFC extension DLL.
`snmp++\binaries\win32\include`	Header files for Win32 SNMP++.
Binaries and Header Files HPUX	
`snmp++\binaries\hpux\snmp++.a`	Shared library for HPUX SNMP++.
`snmp++\binaries\hpux \include`	Header files for HPUX SNMP++.

SNMP++ SNMP Browser for Win32

A complete SNMP browser application is provided that enables you to perform a variety of SNMP tasks. This application and its design are discussed in Chapter 11. The program and source code are provided on the CD-ROM. See Table 10.4.

Table 10.4   **SNMP++ SNMP Browser on CD-ROM.**

CD-ROM Directories and Files	Description
SNMP++ SNMP Browser Application	
`snmp++\browser\source`	Run SETUP.EXE from within this directory to install the complete MSVC++ project for the SNMP++ browser. The setup program will step you through the installation.
`snmp++\browser\application`	Run SETUP.EXE from within this directory to install the SNMP++ browser executable.

IETF SNMP RFCs

In addition to SNMP++ programs and examples, the Internet Engineering Task Force (IETF) Request For Comment (RFC) documents on the SNMP standard also can be found on the CD-ROM. See Table 10.5.

Table 10.5   IETF RFCs on SNMP.

CD-ROM Directories and Files	Description
IETF RFCs on SNMP	
RFCS	Within this directory can be found the latest RFCs on the SNMP standard.

SNMP++ Open Specification Document

The SNMP++ API specification is freely available on the Internet. (See Table 10.6.) A copy of this document also has been provided on the CD-ROM that accompanies this book.

Table 10.6   SNMP++ Open Specification.

CD-ROM Directories and Files	Description
SNMP++ Open Specification	
snmp++/specs/snmp_pp.ps	PostScript format of SNMP++ specification.
snmp++/specs/snmp_pp.doc	MS-Word format of SNMP++ specification.

WinSNMP

SNMP++ utilizes WinSNMP for operation on Win32. (See Table 10.7.) The specification and DLL's for this API are provided on the CD-ROM that accompanies this book.

Table 10.7   WinSnmp Specification.

CD ROM Directories and Files	Description
SNMP++ Open Specification	
winsnmp/winsnmp.doc	MS-Word format of WinSNMP API.
winsnmp/winsnmp.h	Header file for WinSNMP.
winsnmp/winsnmp32.dll	Dynamic link library.
winsnmp/winsnmph32.exe	Helper application.

The winSNMP DLL provided is an evaluation copy from FTP Software, Inc.

[THE PRODUCT IS PROVIDED "AS IS" AND FTP DISCLAIMS ALL WARRANTIES, EXPRESS OR IMPLIED, INCLUDING BUT NOT LIMITED TO THE WARRANTIES OF MERCHANTABILITY AND FITNESS FOR PARTICULAR PURPOSE. FTP DOES NOT WARRANT THAT THE PRODUCT IS ERROR FREE, WILL OPERATE WITHOUT INTERRUPTION, OR IS COMPATIBLE WITH ALL EQUIPMENT AND SOFTWARE CONFIGURATIONS.]

SNMP++ WWW Site

To get the latest information on the SNMP++ API, including source code, examples, and a variety of other information, you can access the SNMP++ Web site at *http://rosegarden.external.hp.com/snmp++*.

REQUIRED TOOLS AND ENVIRONMENT

In order for a reader to utilize the contents of the CD-ROM, a variety of software tools are required. The reader has the option of building the Win32 SNMP++ Dynamic Link Library (DLL) from the provided source or of using the one provided on the CD-ROM. In addition to the SNMP++ DLL, full source code for the SNMP++ browser is included. Microsoft's Visual C++ development environment is required to compile and build either of these packages.

Building the SNMP++ DLL

To build the SNMP++ DLL, the source code on the CD-ROM should be installed on an MS-Windows 32-bit system, MS-Windows 95, or MS-Windows NT. You will need the latest MSVC++ compiler in order to build the library.

Building the SNMP++ Browser Application

To build the SNMP++ Browser application, the source code included on the CD-ROM should be installed on an MS-Windows 32-bit system, MS-Windows 95, or MS-Windows NT. You will need the latest MSVC++ compiler in order to build the library. See Table 10.8.

Table 10.8   Required Environment and Tools.

Required Environment and Tools	Description
SNMP++ CD ROM	CD-ROM that accompanies this book.
MSVC++ Compiler	Microsoft Visual C++ Compiler 4.2 or greater.
Win32 System	Microsoft Windows 32-bit system, MS-Windows 95, or MS-Windows NT.
IP or IPX Configured Protocol Stack	Configure IP or IPX protocol stack on Win32 system.
SNMP agent	At least one SNMP version 1 or version 2 managed agent.

CHAPTER 11

The SNMP++ Browser Application

In this chapter, a working SNMP++ browser is presented that was developed for use with the MS-Windows 32-bit operating systems, including Windows 95 and Windows NT. The browser application performs a variety of valuable SNMP operations, including SNMP Gets, Sets, Get-Nexts, Get-Bulks, Trap sending, and Trap reception. The browser application is examined in detail and the pros and cons of its design are discussed. The browser application in itself can be used as a valuable diagnostic tool when you develop your own management applications. The source code for the browser application included on the CD-ROM that accompanies this book can be used as a basis of designing more complex management applications. See Figure 11.1 on the next page.

All of the examples, user interface, and code illustrated in this chapter come from the SNMP++ browser. It is encouraged that the reader reference the code and program while reading this chapter.

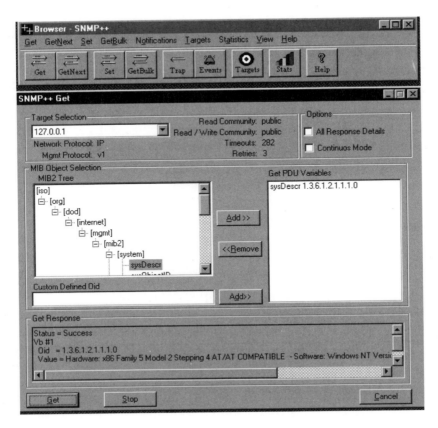

Figure 11.1   SNMP++ Browser Application.

SNMPTARGET MANAGER

In order to manage any entity in SNMP++, an SnmpTarget must be utilized. The SnmpTarget is the encapsulation of a managed entity. For more information, refer to the chapter on SnmpTargets. It is the management application's responsibility to create and manage targets for each entity it manages. A target manager, therefore, is required. The target manager enables the creation, modification, and access of targets. Access of targets by application components that require target information is provided through a target factory.

Target Manager User Interface

The target manager user interface should enable the creation, modification, and deletion of targets. A target is more than just a network address; it also contains information regarding the type of SNMP protocol, an alias name, the retry and time-out values, and the read and write community names. The target user interface provides a centralized interface for the management of targets. Figure 11.2 shows the user interface for creating and editing targets.

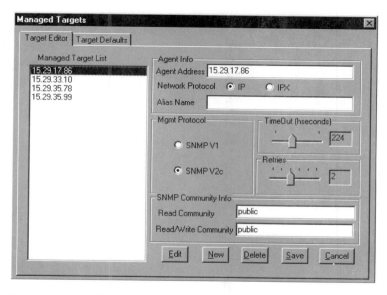

Figure 11.2 SnmpTarget Manager User Interface.

Target Defaults

When SnmpTargets are created, it useful to allow some set of default parameters. Default parameters include definitions of just about everything with the exception of the managed entities network address. See Figure 11.3 on the next page.

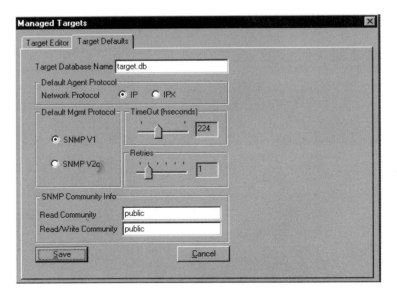

Figure 11.3   Default Target Values.

Target Factory

As targets are created and maintained through the target manager user interface, it is also required to serve targets to application components that require them for management. Rather than push this responsibility on every application component, the target factory is used to make this task easier. The target factory is responsible for manufacturing targets. The target factory handles all the details regarding how a target should be constructed. The consumer of the targets needs to worry only about providing some minimal information about a target (a key); the remainder is handled by the factory. This abstracts the details if a target is an SNMP version 1 or version 2 target. Hence, the target factory facilitates a multilingual interface. In Example 11.1 is the C++ code for a target factory.

Example 11.1   Browser Application Target Factory.

```
SnmpTarget * target_factory( char *key)
{
    CString filename;
    filename = theApp.GetProfileString(  BROWSER_VALUE,
DB_NAME, DEF_DB_NAME);
    // create a target class
    Db target_db;
    TargetDb_Rec db_rec;
    target_db.set_attributtes( filename, sizeof( TargetDb_Rec));

    // read the record
    strcpy( db_rec.key, key);
    if ( target_db.read( &db_rec) == DB_OK)
    {
        CTarget *snmptarget;
        snmptarget = new CTarget( (GenAddress) key);
        snmptarget->set_readcommunity( db_rec.read_community);
        snmptarget->set_writecommunity( db_rec.write_community);
        snmptarget->set_timeout( db_rec.timeout);
        snmptarget->set_retry( db_rec.retries);
        snmptarget->set_version(
                (db_rec.snmp_type == SNMPV1)? version1
: version2c );
        return ( snmptarget);
    }
    else
        return NULL;
};
```

The target factory interfaces with some persistent datastore. The factory attempts to read the requested target based on the provided key. The appropriate target is instantiated and an abstract target (SnmpTarget) is returned.

Alternate Methods of Defining SnmpTargets

A target manager user interface is only one mechanism in which a target can be constructed. More sophisticated management applications can utilize an auto-discovery process in which the target datastore is populated automatically.

PERFORMING AN SNMP++ GET

The most basic and most-used operation in SNMP may be the SNMP Get. (See Figure 11.4.) The Get operation enables you to get an MIB variable when the exact instance in known. A single Get operation may retrieve multiple MIB variables, as many as will fit into a single PDU. The exact number is dependent on the size of each variable retrieved.

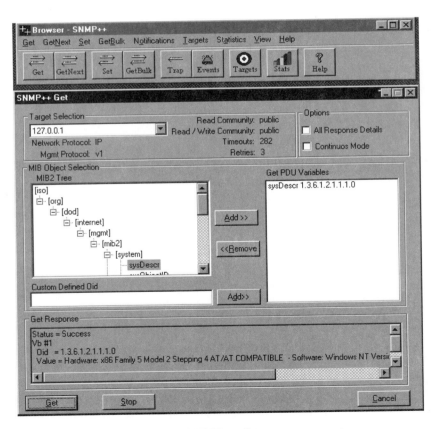

Figure 11.4   Performing an SNMP++ Get.

The Get User Interface

In order to perform a Get, a number of variables must be determined, including the following.

- The target from which to get the MIB variables
- Which MIB variables to get
- What to do with the response
- How to handle errors

Selecting an SnmpTarget

In order to perform a Get, an application should allow the selection of the desired target from which the MIB variables will be retrieved. The previous chapter describes the target interface and target factory. The SNMP++ browser enables the selection of a target from a list of available targets. These are represented as keys to the actual targets. When a user selects a target, the target factory is called and an abstract SnmpTarget is returned. In order to perform an SNMP++ Get, an SnmpTarget object is required.

Selecting an MIB Variable to Get

Once a target has been selected, the MIB objects to be retrieved must be selected. The SNMP++ Get operation, `Snmp::get()`, member function requires an SnmpTarget and a Pdu object. The Pdu object is made up of variable binding objects (Vbs), which are in turn made up of Object Ids (Oids) and values. For the Get operation, the requester need only provide the Oid because the value is returned. The SNMP++ browser allows selection of Oids in two manners.

Selecting an Oid from an MIB Tree

The easiest way to select an MIB object for retrieval is by selecting it from an MIB tree. An MIB tree represents a tree of available objects to retrieve from a specified agent. Since each agent can potentially have its own MIB objects, the tree contents can vary from agent to agent. The SNMP++ browser application provides a set of basic MIB variables that were derived using a basic MIB compiler. The data file that follows in Example 11.2 was derived using an MIB compiler that was then used by the SNMP++ browser application.

Example 11.2   Application of an MIB Table.

```
static char * MIBVals[MAXMIBVALS][3] = {
    "[iso]"                         INDEX,    "1",
    "[org]",                        INDEX,    "1.3",
    "[dod]",                        INDEX,    "1.3.6",
    "[internet]",                   INDEX,    "1.3.6.1",
    "[mgmt]",                       INDEX,    "1.3.6.1.2",
    "[mib2]",                       INDEX,    "1.3.6.1.2.1",
    "[system]",                     INDEX,    "1.3.6.1.2.1.1",
    "sysDescr",                     SCALAR,   "1.3.6.1.2.1.1.1",
    "sysObjectID",                  SCALAR,   "1.3.6.1.2.1.1.2",
    "sysUpTime",                    SCALAR,   "1.3.6.1.2.1.1.3",
    "sysContact",                   SCALAR,   "1.3.6.1.2.1.1.4",
    "sysName",                      SCALAR,   "1.3.6.1.2.1.1.5",
    "sysLocation",                  SCALAR,   "1.3.6.1.2.1.1.6",
    "sysServices",                  SCALAR,   "1.3.6.1.2.1.1.7",
    "[interfaces]",                 SCALAR,   "1.3.6.1.2.1.2",
    "ifNumber",                     SCALAR,   "1.3.6.1.2.1.2.1",
    "[at]",                         INDEX,    "1.3.6.1.2.1.3",
    "[ip]",                         INDEX,    "1.3.6.1.2.1.4",
    "[snmp]",                       INDEX,    "1.3.6.1.2.1.11",
    "snmpInPkts",                   SCALAR,   "1.3.6.1.2.1.11.1",
    "snmpOutPkts",                  SCALAR,   "1.3.6.1.2.1.11.2",
    "snmpInBadversions",            SCALAR,   "1.3.6.1.2.1.11.3",
    "snmpInBadCommunityNames",      SCALAR,   "1.3.6.1.2.1.11.4",
    "snmpInBadCommunityUsers",      SCALAR,   "1.3.6.1.2.1.11.5",
    "snmpInASNParseErrs",           SCALAR,   "1.3.6.1.2.1.11.6",
    "snmpInTooBig",                 SCALAR,   "1.3.6.1.2.1.11.8",
    "snmpInNoSuchNames",            SCALAR,   "1.3.6.1.2.1.11.9",
    "snmpInBadValues",              SCALAR,   "1.3.6.1.2.1.11.10",
    "snmpInReadOnlys",              SCALAR,   "1.3.6.1.2.1.11.11",
    "snmpInGenErrs",                SCALAR,   "1.3.6.1.2.1.11.12",
    "snmpInTotalReqVars",           SCALAR,   "1.3.6.1.2.1.11.13",
    "snmpTotalSetVars",             SCALAR,   "1.3.6.1.2.1.11.14",
    "snmpInGetRequests",            SCALAR,   "1.3.6.1.2.1.11.15",
    "snmpInGetNexts",               SCALAR,   "1.3.6.1.2.1.11.16",
    "snmpInSetRequests",            SCALAR,   "1.3.6.1.2.1.11.17",
    "snmpInGetResponses",           SCALAR,   "1.3.6.1.2.1.11.18",
    "snmpInTraps",                  SCALAR,   "1.3.6.1.2.1.11.19",
    "snmpOutTooBigs",               SCALAR,   "1.3.6.1.2.1.11.20",
    "snmpOutNoSuchNames",           SCALAR,   "1.3.6.1.2.1.11.21",
```

```
"snmpOutBadValues",        SCALAR,    "1.3.6.1.2.1.11.22",
"snmpOutGenErrs",          SCALAR,    "1.3.6.1.2.1.11.24",
"snmpOutGetRequests",      SCALAR,    "1.3.6.1.2.1.11.25",
"snmpOutGetNexts",         SCALAR,    "1.3.6.1.2.1.11.26",
"snmpOutSetRequests",      SCALAR,    "1.3.6.1.2.1.11.27",
"snmpOutgetResponses",     SCALAR,    "1.3.6.1.2.1.11.28",
"snmpOutTraps",            SCALAR,    "1.3.6.1.2.1.11.29",
"snmpEnableAuthenTraps",   SCALAR,    "1.3.6.1.2.1.11.30" };
```

The table generated by an MIB compiler creates three columns of data. The first column denotes the friendly name associated with an MIB Oid. The second column denotes whether or not the Oid is a scalar or an index. Scalar objects represent instances, and indexes are used for navigational purposes only and do not represent objects that can be retrieved. The last column denotes the actual MIB Oid. Once generated, a program can use the data to construct a user interface, as shown in Figure 11.5 on the next page.

Defining a Custom Oid   In addition to allowing MIB object selection from a predefined tree, a flexible user interface should allow definition of custom Oids. This enables you to get objects that were not compiled as part of the MIB.

Issuing an Asynchronous Get Method

Once a target and Pdu payload have been selected, an SNMP++ Get can be invoked. The SNMP++ browser application utilizes asynchronous mode for Get transactions. The C++ code for issuing the asynchronous Get is as follows in Example 11.3, shown on page 205.

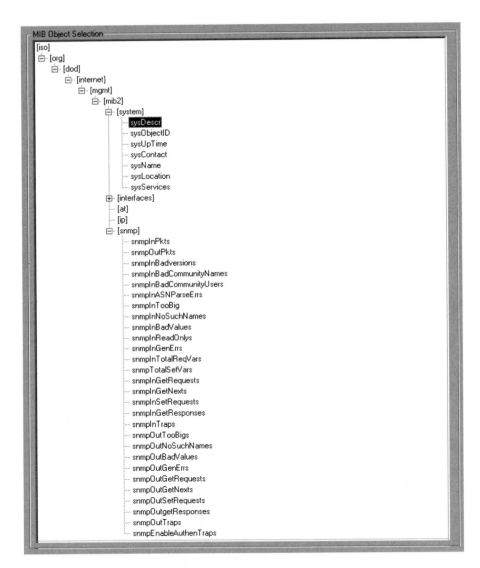

Figure 11.5   Machine-Generated MIB UI.

Example 11.3   Application Issuing an SNMP++ Get.

```
void Get::OnGet()   {
    CListBox *lb; int count;
    char buffer[80],*ptr, key[80];;
    Pdu pdu;                                  // SNMP++ Pdu object

    lb = ( CListBox*) GetDlgItem( IDC_PDU);     // get the ListBox id
    if ( (count=lb->GetCount()) <1) {           // make sure we have
                                                // something to get
        AfxMessageBox("There are No PDU Variables to Get");
        return;  }

    for ( int z =0;z<count;z++) {               // build up an SNMP++ Pdu
        lb->GetText(z,buffer);                  // get the text from the listbox
        ptr = buffer;                           // get rid of the text part
        while (*ptr != ' ') ptr++;
            ptr++;
        Oid oid( ptr);                          // make an SNMP++ Oid
        Vb vb( oid);                            // make an SNMP++ Vb with the Oid
        pdu += vb; }                            // add the vb to the Pdu

        CComboBox *cb
        = ( CComboBox *) GetDlgItem( IDC_TARGETS);     // make an SnmpTarget

        if ( cb->GetCurSel() == CB_ERR) {
            AfxMessageBox("No Target Selected!");
            return; }

        cb->GetLBText( cb->GetCurSel(), key);
        SnmpTarget *target = target_factory( key); // get a target from the
                                                    // target factory
        if ( target == NULL) {
            AfxMessageBox("Unable To find Target");
            return; }

        int status = snmp->get( pdu,            // Invoke an SNMP++ Get
                        *target,
                        (snmp_callback) &my_getcallback,
                        (void *) this);

        if ( status != SNMP_CLASS_SUCCESS)
            AfxMessageBox( snmp->error_msg( status));

        m_output = "SNMP++ Get In Progress...";    // clear the output display
            UpdateData( FALSE);

        delete target;                          // free up the target when complete

        enable_controls( FALSE);  // disable all controls while get is pending
};
```

The SNMP++ Get code in Example 11.3 was developed to integrate with Microsoft's Visual C++ and Microsoft Foundation Classes. The code cooperates with a number of GUI controls, including a listbox in which all the selected Oids are stored. The `Snmp::get()` call passes in the target returned from the target factory and the built-up Pdu object. In addition, the address of the callback function and optional callback data are used. For the callback data a pointer to *this* is specified. *This* denotes a self reference to the current MFC dialog object. When the callback function is fired, the callback data is used to point back and reference the MFC object that made the call.

Receiving a Get Response via Callback Function

The specified callback function is used to handle all asynchronous responses. In addition to responses, a time-out message can be generated as well. The callback function is defined as follows in Example 11.4.

Example 11.4   Browser Application Get Response Callback Function.

```
void my_getcallback( int reason,
                     Snmp* snmp,
                     Pdu &pdu,
                     SnmpTarget &target,
                     void * callback_data)
{
   Get * get_window = (Get *) callback_data;    // resolve the callback data
                                                 // to a MFC Get Window Handle
   CButton * continue_mode = (CButton*) get_window->GetDlgItem
                     ( IDC_CONTINUOS);

   switch ( reason)                      // based on the reason handle the reason
   {
      case SNMP_CLASS_ASYNC_RESPONSE:            // an asynchronous response
                                                 // has arrived
      {
         get_window->display_response( pdu, target, snmp);
         if (( continue_mode->GetCheck()) && (pdu.get_error_status()== 0))
         get_window->get_another();
         else
            get_window->enable_controls( TRUE);}
         break;

      case SNMP_CLASS_TIMEOUT:                   // a timeout has occured
```

```
            get_window->display_timeout( target);
            get_window->enable_controls( TRUE);
        break;

    }                                                // end switch
};
```

The callback function resolves the callback data to point to the calling MFC dialog object. It can then use the pointer to call back the MFC object to process the response. The callback function handles two cases, a response or a time-out. In the event a response is received, the callback calls the display_response() member function. If a time-out is generated, the display_timeout() member function is invoked.

Displaying the Get Response

Once a response has been called to the callback and the callback function has called the display_response() member function, the payload of the response Pdu object is displayed, as shown in Example 11.5

Example 11.5   Displaying an Asynchronous Get Response.

```
{

    GenAddress address;                      // SNMP++ generic Address
    Vb vb;
    int error_status = pdu.get_error_status();
    char buffer[50];

    m_output = "Status = ";                   // show the result status
    m_output += snmp->error_msg( error_status);
    m_output += "\r\n";

    CButton * all_details = (CButton*) GetDlgItem( IDC_ALL_DETAILS);
    if ( all_details->GetCheck())
    {
        target.get_address( address);
        m_output += "Response from ";
            m_output += address.get_printable();
            m_output += "\r\n";
```

(continued)

Example 11.5   *(continued)*

```
        m_output += "Error Status = ";
            m_output += snmp->error_msg( error_status );
            m_output += "\r\n";
        sprintf( buffer,"Error Index  = %d\r\n", pdu.get_error_index());
        m_output += buffer;
            printf( buffer,"Request ID = %ld\r\n",pdu.get_request_id());
            m_output += buffer;
        sprintf( buffer,"Variable Binding Count =
                %d\r\n",pdu.get_vb_count());
        m_output += buffer;
    }

    for ( int x=0;x<pdu.get_vb_count();x++)   // show the Vbs
    {
        pdu.get_vb( vb,x);
            sprintf( buffer,"Vb #%d\r\n",x+1);
            m_output += buffer;
            m_output += "  Oid   = ";
            m_output += vb.get_printable_oid();
            m_output += "\r\n";
            m_output += "  Value = ";
            m_output += vb.get_printable_value();
            m_output += "\r\n";
    }
    UpdateData( FALSE);                        // update the output display
};
```

PERFORMING AN SNMP++ SET

The SNMP Set operation enables you to set MIB object instances to manager-provided values. (See Figure 11.6.) When MIB objects are defined in an MIB definition, their attributes are also defined. These attributes determine a number of things, including whether or not an MIB object is readable, writeable, and what SMI data type it holds. In order to set an MIB object, the object must be writeable and a valid SMI value must be provided. (In addition to this, the appropriate community name also must be provided.) In the event an object is not writeable or if the SMI value is not valid, an error is generated.

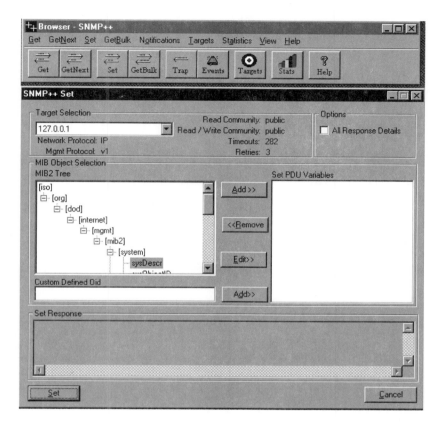

Figure 11.6   Performing an SNMP++ Set.

The Set User Interface

In order to perform a Set, a number of variables must be determined, including the following.

- Which target to set the MIB variables
- Which MIB variables to set
- For each MIB variable, the value to be used
- What to do with the response
- How to handle errors

Selecting an SnmpTarget

A browser that enables Sets should enable you to select the desired target for the MIB variables. The SNMP++ browser enables you to select a target from a list of available targets. These are represented as keys to the actual targets. When a user selects a target, the target factory is called and an abstract SnmpTarget is returned. In order to perform an SNMP++ Set, an SnmpTarget object is required.

Selecting an MIB Variable to Set

Once a target has been selected, the MIB objects to be set must be selected. The SNMP++ Set operations, `Snmp::set()`, member function requires an SnmpTarget and a Pdu object. The Pdu object is made up of variable binding objects (Vbs), which in turn are made up of Object Ids (Oids) and values. For the Set operation, the requester needs to provide the Oid and the set value. See Figure 11.7.

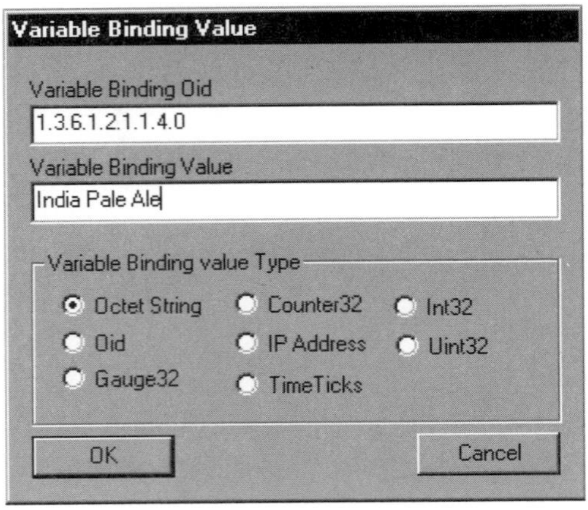

Figure 11.7   Setting an MIB Value.

Issuing a Blocked Mode Set Method

Once a target and Pdu payload have been assembled, an SNMP++ Set can be invoked. The SNMP++ browser application utilizes blocked mode for Set transactions. The C++ code for issuing the blocked mode set is as follows in Example 11.6.

Example 11.6   Browser Application Issuing a Blocked Mode Set.

```
void Set::OnSet()
{
   CListBox *lb;
   lb = ( CListBox*) GetDlgItem( IDC_PDU);
   Pdu pdu;
   char key[80];

   int vb_count = lb->GetCount();            // determine the number of
                                             // Vbs to Set

   if ( vb_count == 0) {
     AfxMessageBox("You have No Variable Bindings to Set");
     return;   }

   pdu.set_vblist( set_vbs, vb_count);       // set the vbs into the Pdu

   CComboBox *cb = ( CComboBox *) GetDlgItem( IDC_TARGETS);   // make
                                an SnmpTarget using the Target_Factory
    if ( cb->GetCurSel() == CB_ERR) {
      AfxMessageBox("No Target Selected!");
      return; }
   cb->GetLBText( cb->GetCurSel(), key);     // get the currently
                                             // selected target key

   SnmpTarget *target = target_factory( key);  // get a target from
                                               // the target factory
   if ( target == NULL) {
     AfxMessageBox("Unable To find Target");
     return };

   m_output = "";                            // clear the output display
   UpdateData( FALSE);

   int status = snmp->set( pdu,  *target);   // Invoke an SNMP++ Get
                                             // for the Pdu requested

   display_response( status, pdu, *target, snmp);  // display response
}
```

PERFORMING AN SNMP++ GET-NEXT

The SNMP Get-Next operation enables you to retrieve MIB variables where the exact instance of the variable to retrieve is not specified. Get-Next retrieves the next instance of the requested MIB object. This is useful when you retrieve MIB variables and the exact instance is not known, such as when reading tables. SNMP++ supports a Get-Next interface for both blocked and asynchronous modes. In order to perform a Get-Next using SNMP++, a target and Pdu must be specified. The target is similar to usage in other SNMP++ requests. The Pdu holds the variables to be retrieved via Get-Next. See Figure 11.8.

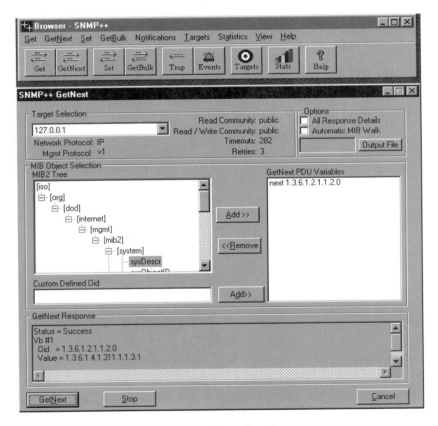

Figure 11.8   Performing an SNMP++ Get-Next.

The Get-Next User Interface

The Get-Next user interface enables you to select MIB variables to Get-Next on. A single Pdu can have multiple Get-Next variables in which an agent performs a Get-Next on each variable and returns the result in the response Pdu. Returned will be the next MIB object instance for each variable requested. For example, assume we are performing a Get-Next on an MIB Oid of "1." Returned will be the next MIB object instance, probably the sysDescr (system descriptor 1.3.6.1.2.1.1.1.0) object. If the request Pdu contains more than one variable, then the Get-Next response contains a response variable for each request variable. For example, assume we have a Get-Next request Pdu with three variables, "1," "1," and "1." Returned are three sysDescr objects.

Selecting an SnmpTarget

A browser that supports Get-Nexts should enable you to select the desired target from which to Get-Next the MIB variables. The SNMP++ browser enables you to select a target from a list of available targets. These are represented as keys to the actual targets. When a user has selected a target, the target factory is called and an abstract SnmpTarget is returned. In order to perform an SNMP++ Get-Next, an SnmpTarget object is required.

Selecting MIB Variables to Get-Next

Similar to the Get operation, the Get-Next operation enables you to select MIB objects from an MIB tree or a custom object. Unlike the browser SNMP++ Get dialog box for which only scalars can be selected, using Get-Next one can select either an *index* or *scalar* object. Since Get-Next returns the next object, if one selects an *index* the first instance following that index is returned.

Issuing the Get-Next Method

Once a target and Pdu payload are selected, an SNMP++ Get-Next can be invoked. The SNMP++ browser application utilizes asynchronous mode for Get-Next transactions. The C++ code for issuing the asynchronous Get is as follows in Example 11.7 on the next page.

Example 11.7   Browser Application Issuing a Get-Next Method.

```
void GetNext::OnGetnext()
{
   CListBox *lb;
   int count;
   char buffer[80],*ptr;   Pdu pdu;

   lb = ( CListBox*) GetDlgItem( IDC_PDU);   // get the ListBox id
   if ( (count=lb->GetCount()) <1) {         // make sure we have
                                             // something to get
      AfxMessageBox("There are No PDU Variables to GetNext");
      return;
   }

   for ( int z =0;z<count;z++) {        // build up an SNMP++ Pdu
      lb->GetText(z,buffer);            // get the text from the listbox
      ptr = buffer;                     // get rid of the text part
      while (*ptr != ' ') ptr++;
       ptr++;
      Oid oid( ptr);                    // make an SNMP++ Oid
      Vb vb( oid);                      // make an SNMP++ Vb with the oid
      pdu += vb;                        // add the vb to the Pdu
      }


      CComboBox *cb = ( CComboBox *) GetDlgItem( IDC_TARGETS);
      char key[80];
      if ( cb->GetCurSel() == CB_ERR)   {
         AfxMessageBox("No Target Selected!");
         return;
      }
      cb->GetLBText( cb->GetCurSel(), key);
      SnmpTarget *target = target_factory( key); // get a target from
                                                 // the target factory

      if ( target == NULL) {
         AfxMessageBox("Unable To find Target");
         return;
      }

      int status = snmp->get_next( pdu,     // Invoke an SNMP++ GetNext
                                   *target,
                                   (snmp_callback) &my_getnextcallback,
                                   (void *) this);

      if ( status != SNMP_CLASS_SUCCESS)
         AfxMessageBox( snmp->error_msg( status));

      delete target;                       // free up the target
      enable_controls( FALSE);             // disable all controls
}
```

Receiving a Get-Next Response via a Callback Function

The specified callback function is used to handle all asynchronous responses. In addition to responses, a time-out message can be generated as well. The callback function is defined as follows in Example 11.8.

Example 11.8   Browser Application Get-Next Callback Function.

```
void my_getnextcallback( int reason,
                         Snmp* snmp,
                         Pdu &pdu,
                         SnmpTarget &target,
void * callback_data)
{
   GetNext * getnext_window = (GetNext *) callback_data;  // resolve
                                                         // to a MFC Handle
   CButton * mib_walk =                  // determine if we are in auto
                                         // walk mode
            (CButton*) getnext_window->GetDlgItem( IDC_AUTOWALK);

   switch ( reason)                      // based on the reason handle
                                         // the reason
   {
      case SNMP_CLASS_ASYNC_RESPONSE:    // an asynchronous response
                                         // has arrived
         getnext_window->display_response( pdu, target, snmp);
         if (( mib_walk->GetCheck()) &&(pdu.get_error_status()==0))
            getnext_window->getnext_another();
         else
            getnext_window->enable_controls( TRUE);
      break;

      case SNMP_CLASS_TIMEOUT:           // a timeout has occured
         getnext_window->display_timeout( target);
         getnext_window->enable_controls( TRUE);
      break;

   } // end switch
};
```

The callback function resolves the callback data to point to the calling MFC dialog object. It can then use the pointer to call back into the MFC object to process the response. The callback function handles two cases, a response or a time-out. In the event a response is received, the callback calls the `display_response()` member function. If a time-out is generated, the `display_timeout()` member function is invoked.

Displaying the Get-Next Response

Once a response has been called to the callback and the callback function has called the `display_response()` member function, the payload of the response Pdu object is displayed. The code in Example 11.9 iterates through the response Pdu and displays the result.

Example 11.9   Browser Application Displaying Get-Next Response.

```
void GetNext::display_response(Pdu &pdu,SnmpTarget &target, Snmp *snmp)
{
   GenAddress address;                        // SNMP++ generic Address
   char buffer[150];
   Vb vb;
   int error_status = pdu.get_error_status();
   m_output = "Status = ";                     // show the result status
   m_output += snmp->error_msg( error_status);
   m_output += "\r\n";

   CButton * all_details = (CButton*) GetDlgItem( IDC_ALL_DETAILS);
   if ( all_details->GetCheck())   {
      target.get_address( address);
      m_output += "Response from ";
         m_output += address.get_printable();
         m_output += "\r\n";
      sprintf( buffer,"Error Status = %d, %s\r\n",
              pdu.get_error_status(),
              snmp->error_msg(pdu.get_error_status())));
      m_output += buffer;
      sprintf( buffer,"Error Index  = %d\r\n", pdu.get_error_index());
      m_output += buffer;
         sprintf( buffer,"Request ID = %ld\r\n",pdu.get_request_id());
         m_output += buffer;
      sprintf( buffer,"Variable Binding Count = %d\r\n",
                                          pdu.get_vb_count());
      m_output += buffer;
   }
```

```
CListBox *lb;                                  // clear the pdu selection box
lb = ( CListBox*) GetDlgItem( IDC_PDU);
lb->ResetContent();
for ( int x=0;x<pdu.get_vb_count();x++)   {
    pdu.get_vb( vb,x);
        sprintf( buffer,"Vb #%d\r\n",x+1);
        m_output += buffer;
        m_output += "   Oid   = ";
        m_output += vb.get_printable_oid();
        m_output += "\r\n";
        m_output += "   Value = ";
        m_output += vb.get_printable_value();
        m_output += "\r\n";

        CString nextoid;    // update each vb in the Pdu selection box
        nextoid = "next ";
        nextoid += vb.get_printable_oid();
        lb->InsertString( lb->GetCount(),nextoid);
    }
    UpdateData( FALSE);        // update the output display
};
```

Invoking Multiple Get-Nexts

When performing Get-Nexts, it is possible to walk an agent's MIB automatically by using the response MIB variable as the next request. An entire agent's MIB can be walked, one variable at a time, in this manner. The browser application allows invoking automatic Get-Nexts optionally, so that when it is selected, a new request Pdu is constructed from the previous response. This continues until an error occurs. For SNMP version 1 agents, a "no such name" error is generated when the end of MIB is encountered. SNMP version 2 agents return an explicit error code for "end of MIB view."

PERFORMING AN SNMP++ GET-BULK

The SNMP Get-Bulk operation enables you to perform bulk retrieval of
MIB variables using the standard SNMP Get-Bulk operation. Get-Bulk
vastly increases the performance of retrieving MIB variables and is especially useful when dealing with tables. SNMP++ supports a bilingual
interface that enables you to use the Get-Bulk interface over SNMP version 1 agents that do not support Get-Bulk. For these agents, Get-Bulk is
mapped over the Get-Next operation. See Figure 11.9.

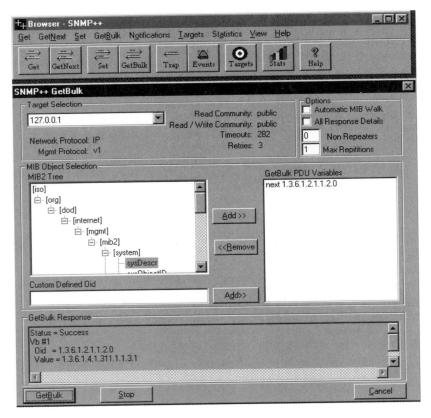

Figure 11.9   Performing an SNMP++ Get-Bulk.

The Get-Bulk User Interface

The Get-Bulk user interface enables you to select MIB variables on which to Get-Bulk. The user can select MIB variables for bulk retrieval and can select those variables that are "non-repeaters" and that are "max repetitions." Non-repeaters are variable bindings that are at the start of a Pdu and should be retrieved without repetition. The SNMP++ browser enables you to define the "non-repeaters" value from zero to ten. Maximum repetitions define variable bindings beyond the non-repeaters that will be retrieved in iteration.

Selecting an SnmpTarget

A browser that enables Get-Bulks should also enable you to select the desired target from which to Get-Bulk the MIB variables. The SNMP++ browser enables you to select a target from a list of available targets. These are represented as keys to the actual targets. When a user selects a target, the target factory is called and an abstract SnmpTarget is returned. In order to perform an SNMP++ Get-Bulk, an SnmpTarget object is required.

Issuing the Get-Bulk Method

Once a target and Pdu payload are selected, an SNMP++ Get-Bulk may be invoked. The SNMP++ browser application utilizes asynchronous mode for Get-Next transactions. The C++ code for issuing the asynchronous Get is as shown in Example 11.10 on the next page.

Example 11.10   Browser Application Issuing a Get-Bulk Method.

```
void GetBulk::OnGetbulk()
{
   CListBox *lb;
   int count;
   char buffer[80],*ptr;
   Pdu pdu;                                          // SNMP++ Pdu object

   UpdateData( TRUE );                         // update data to get non
                                               // repeaters and max repss
   lb = ( CListBox*) GetDlgItem( IDC_PDU);     // get the ListBox id
     if ( (count=lb->GetCount()) <1) {         // make sure we have
                                               // something to get
       AfxMessageBox("There are No PDU Variables to GetBulk");
       return;
   }

   for ( int z =0;z<count;z++) {               // build up an SNMP++
                                               // Pdu with all the Vbs

     // get the text from the listbox
     lb->GetText(z,buffer);
     ptr = buffer;                             // get rid of the text part
     while (*ptr != ' ') ptr++;
        ptr++;
     Oid oid( ptr);     // make an SNMP++ Oid with the dotted notation
     Vb vb( oid);                         // make an SNMP++ Vb with the oid
     pdu += vb;                           // add the vb to the Pdu
   }

   CComboBox *cb = ( CComboBox *) GetDlgItem( IDC_TARGETS);
   char key[80];
   if ( cb->GetCurSel() == CB_ERR) {
      AfxMessageBox("No Target Selected!");
      return;
   }
   cb->GetLBText( cb->GetCurSel(), key);

   SnmpTarget *target = target_factory( key);   // get a target from
                                                // the target factory

   if ( target == NULL) {
      AfxMessageBox("Unable To find Target");
      return;
   }

   int status = snmp->get_bulk( pdu,                // Invoke an SNMP++ Get
                                                    // for the Pdu requested
                          *target,
                          m_non_repeaters,
                          m_max_repititions,
                          (snmp_callback) &my_getbulkcallback,
                          (void *) this);
```

```
if ( status != SNMP_CLASS_SUCCESS)
   AfxMessageBox( snmp->error_msg( status));

delete target;              // free up the target when complete
enable_controls( FALSE);    // disable all controls while get is
                            // pending
}
```

Receiving a Get-Bulk Response via a Callback Function

The specified callback function is used to handle all asynchronous responses. In addition to responses, a time-out message can be generated as well. The callback function is defined as follows in Example 11.11.

Example 11.11   Browser Application Get-Bulk Callback Function.

```
void my_getbulkcallback( int reason,
                         Snmp* snmp,
                         Pdu &pdu,
                         SnmpTarget &target,
                         void * callback_data)
{
    GetBulk * getbulk_window = (GetBulk *) callback_data;  // resolve
                             // the callback data to a MFC Handle
    CButton * mib_walk =
        (CButton*) getbulk_window->GetDlgItem( IDC_AUTOWALK);

    switch ( reason)         // based on the reason handle the reason
    {
    case SNMP_CLASS_ASYNC_RESPONSE:      // an asynchronous response has
                                         // arrived
    getbulk_window->display_response( pdu, target, snmp);

    if (( mib_walk->GetCheck()) &&(pdu.get_error_status()==0)) // look
                                        // for continuos mode
        getbulk_window->getbulk_another();
    else
        getbulk_window->enable_controls( TRUE);
    break;

    case SNMP_CLASS_TIMEOUT:                     // a timeout has occured
        getbulk_window->display_timeout( target);
        getbulk_window->enable_controls( TRUE);
    break;

    } // end switch
};
```

The callback function resolves the callback data to point to the calling MFC dialog object. It can then use the pointer to call back into the MFC object to process the response. The callback function handles two cases, a response or a time-out. In the event a response is received, the callback calls the `display_response()` member function. If a time-out is generated, the `display_timeout()` member function is invoked.

Displaying the Get-Bulk Response

Once a response is posted to the callback and the callback function calls the `display_response()`, the payload of the response Pdu object is displayed. See Example 11.12.

Example 11.12   Browser Application Displaying Get-Bulk Response.

```
void GetBulk::display_response( Pdu &pdu,SnmpTarget &target,Snmp *snmp)
{
   GenAddress address;                      // SNMP++ generic Address
   char buffer[150];
   Vb vb;
   int error_status = pdu.get_error_status();
   m_output = "Status = ";                  // show the result status
   m_output += snmp->error_msg( error_status);
   m_output += "\r\n";

   CButton * all_details = (CButton*) GetDlgItem( IDC_ALL_DETAILS);
   if ( all_details->GetCheck())
   {
      target.get_address( address);
      m_output += "Response from ";
      m_output += address.get_printable();
      m_output += "\r\n";
      sprintf( buffer,"Error Status=%d, %s\r\n",pdu.get_error_status(),
               snmp->error_msg(pdu.get_error_status()));
      m_output += buffer;
      sprintf( buffer,"Error Index  = %d\r\n", pdu.get_error_index());
      m_output += buffer;
      sprintf( buffer,"Request ID = %ld\r\n",pdu.get_request_id());
      m_output += buffer;
      sprintf( buffer,"Variable Binding Count = %d\r\n",
                                          pdu.get_vb_count());
      m_output += buffer;
   }
```

```
CListBox *lb;                          // clear the pdu selection box
lb = ( CListBox*) GetDlgItem( IDC_PDU);
lb->ResetContent();

for ( int x=0;x<pdu.get_vb_count();x++)        // show the Vbs
{
    pdu.get_vb( vb,x);
        sprintf( buffer,"Vb #%d\r\n",x+1);
        m_output += buffer;
        m_output += "  Oid   = ";
        m_output += vb.get_printable_oid();
        m_output += "\r\n";
        m_output += "  Value = ";
        m_output += vb.get_printable_value();
        m_output += "\r\n";
        CString nextoid;                   // update each vb
        nextoid = "next ";
        nextoid += vb.get_printable_oid();
        lb->InsertString( lb->GetCount(),nextoid);
}
    UpdateData( FALSE);                    // update the output display
};
```

SENDING NOTIFICATIONS WITH SNMP++

SNMP++ supports sending of both traps and notifications through the API. This is useful where a management station would like to notify another management station or notify itself (via loopback) through the trap interface. Sending a trap is an asynchronous event; there is no expected response Pdu. SNMP++ supports an SNMP version 2 view of traps. That is, trap identifiers and enterprise-specific values are represented as Oids. The browser application user interface is similar to the other SNMP++ functions in that a target and Pdu are required. When you create a Pdu, however, a few other parameters must be set. These include the identity, enterprise, and time stamp for the trap. See Figure 11.10 on the next page.

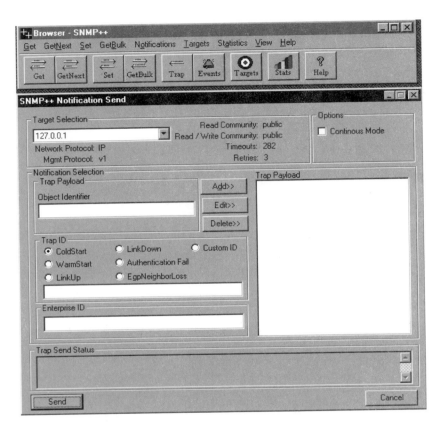

Figure 11.10   Sending Notifications.

The Notification Send User Interface

The Notification Send user interface enables you to select MIB variables to send. Along with the Oid for each variable, the user can also define the value of the variable binding. The trap payload holds as many variable bindings as will be excepted by an agent listening on the trap port. See Figure 11.11.

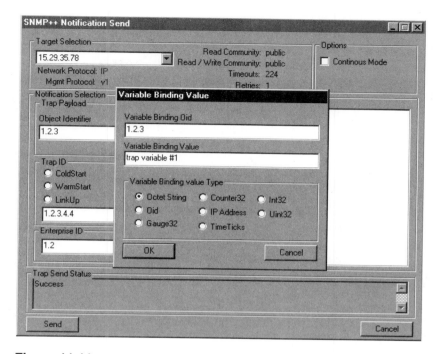

Figure 11.11   Definition of the Trap Payload Variable Binding.

In addition to adding MIB variables to the trap payload, the identification and enterprise of the trap can be defined. The trap ID is an Oid that defines the type of trap to be sent. Traps can take a variety of IDs, including well-known IDs and custom ones.

- **Trap Identification.**   Generic trap IDs include ColdStart, WarmStart, LinkUp, LinkDown, Authentication failure, and EgpNeighborloss. If the trap type does not fall into this set, a custom Oid can be defined (custom is defined to be any Oid not in this set).

- **Enterprise.**   All traps may also have an enterprise. The browser user interface enables you to define an enterprise Oid that will be included with the trap.

Selecting an SnmpTarget

A browser that enables trap sending should allow you to select the desired target to which to send the trap. The SNMP++ browser enables you to select a target from a list of available targets. These are represented as keys to the actual targets. When a user selects a target, the target factory is called and an abstract SnmpTarget is returned. In order to perform an SNMP++ Trap Send, an SnmpTarget object is required. See Example 11.13.

Example 11.13   Browser Application Sending a Trap.

```
void NotifySend::OnSend()
{
    Oid trapid; Pdu trap_pdu; char buffer[200]; char key[80]; int
      trap_type;
    UpdateData( TRUE );                          // update MFC variables
    trap_type = GetCheckedRadioButton( IDC_RCOLDSTART,  IDC_RCUSTOM);

      switch( trap_type)  {
    case IDC_RCOLDSTART:
          trapid = coldStart; break;
    case IDC_RWARMSTART:
          trapid = warmStart; break;
    case IDC_RLINKUP:
          trapid = linkUp; break;
    case IDC_RLINKDOWN:
          trapid = linkDown; break;
    case IDC_RAUTHFAIL:
          trapid = authenticationFailure; break;
    case IDC_REGPLOSS:
          trapid = egpNeighborLoss; break;
    case IDC_RCUSTOM: {
        strcpy( buffer, m_customid);
        Oid coid( buffer);
        if ( !coid.valid()) {
            AfxMessageBox("Invalid Custom Oid"); return; }
        trapid =  coid;   } }            // end switch
    trap_pdu.set_notify_id( trapid);       // attach the id to the pdu
    strcpy( buffer, m_enterprise);         // determine the enterprise
    Oid enterprise_oid( buffer);
    trap_pdu.set_notify_enterprise( enterprise_oid);
    CComboBox *cb = ( CComboBox *) GetDlgItem( IDC_TARGETS);
    if ( cb->GetCurSel() == CB_ERR) {
        AfxMessageBox("No Target Selected!");
        return; }
    cb->GetLBText( cb->GetCurSel(), key);
```

```
   SnmpTarget *target = target_factory( key);    // get a target
   if ( target == NULL) {
      AfxMessageBox("Unable To find Target");
      return; }
   CListBox *lb;                                  // build up the payload
   lb = ( CListBox*) GetDlgItem( IDC_PDU);
   for (int x=0;x<lb->GetCount();x++)
         trap_pdu += trap_vbs[x];
 m_output = "";                                   // clear output display
   UpdateData( FALSE);
   int status = snmp->trap( trap_pdu, *target);// send the trap
   m_output = snmp->error_msg( status);     // display trap send status
   if ( status == SNMP_CLASS_SUCCESS) {     // look for continuos mode
      CButton * continue_mode = (CButton*) GetDlgItem( IDC_CONTINUOS);
    if ( continue_mode->GetCheck())
         SetTimer(100,500,NULL); }
   delete target;                                // free up the target
}
```

RECEIVING NOTIFICATIONS WITH SNMP++

SNMP+ enables an application to receive notifications and to apply simple filtering. The browser application implements a simple user interface for the reception, filtering, and display of notifications. Because trap ports are a shared resource of SNMP++, multiple instances of the notification reception window can exist, each with their own unique set of filtering parameters. Notifications are asynchronous events. That is, a notification can come in at any time. The browser application enables traps to arrive over IP- and/or IPX-based addresses on the protocol stack installed on your MS-Windows system. Both of these transports utilize well-known port/socket numbers for trap reception. See Figure 11.12 on the next page.

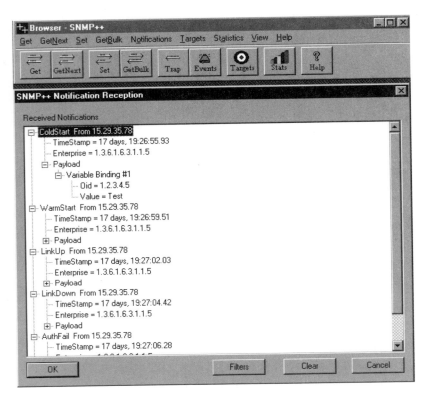

Figure 11.12   Notification Reception.

Notification Receive User Interface

The user interface is simple. Trap registration and filtering begin automatically when the MFC dialog box is instantiated. Each notification arrives as an MFC tree control element that can be expanded or collapsed to display the details of any notification. This enables you to easily view the type of notification, the time it arrived, and its enterprise and variable binding payload.

Registering for Notifications

The SNMP++ code that follows in Example 11.14 registers for the reception of notifications. The `Snmp::notify_register()` member function is invoked within the constructor for the MFC dialog class.

Example 11.14   Browser Application Registering for Notifications.

```
NotifyReceive::NotifyReceive(CWnd* pParent /*=NULL*/)
       : CDialog(NotifyReceive::IDD, pParent)
{
   //{{AFX_DATA_INIT(NotifyReceive)
   // NOTE: the ClassWizard will add member initialization here
   //}}AFX_DATA_INIT

   int cstatus = Create(IDD, pParent);


   int status;
   TargetCollection targets;        // empty get all from all targets
   snmp = new Snmp( status);        // create an snmp++ object
   if ( status != SNMP_CLASS_SUCCESS)
   {
      AfxMessageBox("Unable To Create Snmp Object!");
      snmp = NULL;
   }

   Oid coldStart("1.3.6.1.6.3.1.1.5.1");            // start out with all
                                                    // filters enabled
   my_filters += coldStart;
   Oid warmStart("1.3.6.1.6.3.1.1.5.2");
   my_filters += warmStart;
   Oid linkUp("1.3.6.1.6.3.1.1.5.3");
   my_filters += linkUp;
   Oid linkDown("1.3.6.1.6.3.1.1.5.4");
   my_filters += linkDown;
   Oid authenticationFailure("1.3.6.1.6.3.1.1.5.5");
   my_filters += authenticationFailure;
   Oid egpNeighborLoss("1.3.6.1.6.3.1.1.5.6");
   my_filters += egpNeighborLoss;

   status = snmp->notify_register( my_filters,targets, // register to
                                                       // receive traps
                              (snmp_callback) &my_trap_callback,
                              (void *) this);
   if ( status != SNMP_CLASS_SUCCESS)
      AfxMessageBox("Unable to Regsiter For Traps");

}
```

Notification Filtering

The notification dialog box enables you to filter out specific types of traps. This is based on the ID of the trap. SNMP++ enables additional filtering, but for the sake of simplicity only minimal filtering is provided within the browser application. See Figure 11.13

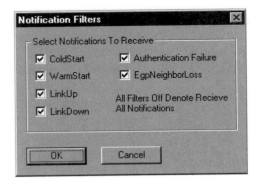

Figure 11.13   Notification Filtering.

Glossary of Acronyms

ADT (Abstract Data Type) An ADT is a data type that encapsulates the data and behavior of an object in an abstract manner.

API (Application Programmers Interface) APIs are the basis of interaction between a program and some predefined library.

ASN.1 (Abstract Syntax Notation 1) The syntax used when describing language within OSI.

BER (Basic Encoding Rules) The syntax used when describing data transfer within OSI.

BOF (Birds of a Feather) An informal round table discussion.

CPU (Central Processing Unit) The main processing unit of a computer.

CMIP (Common Management Information Protocol) The OSI protocol for network management.

CMIS (Common Management Information Service) The service provided by CMIP.

CMOT (CMIP over TCP) OSI management protocol and framework using Internet suite of protocols.

DMI (Desktop Management Interface) The interface for desktop management as defined by the DMTF.

DMTF (Desktop Management Task Force) A de facto task force concerned with the management of desktop systems, including PCs, servers, and printers.

GUI (Graphical User Interface)   A user interface that is represented using graphics and most typically driven using a mouse.

IAB (Internet Architecture Board)   The technical group overlooking the development of protocols within the Internet.

IANA (Internet Assigned Numbers Authority)   The authority within the Internet responsible for assigning numbers specific to Internet-related protocols.

IEEE (Institute of Electrical and Electronics Engineers)   A standards body responsible for defining and maintaining standards in regard to electrical and electronics equipment.

IETF (Internet Engineering Task Force)   A task force of the IAB that is responsible for short-term and immediate needs and goals.

IP (Internet Protocol)   The common term used to refer to the TCP/IP suite of protocols.

IPng (Internet Protocol Next Generation, a.k.a. IP version 6)   The next generation of the IP protocol that addresses many of the deficiencies of IP version 4.

IPX (Internet Packet Exchange)   A common local area protocol developed by Novell, Inc.

IRTF (Internet Research Task Force)   A task force of the IAB concerned with longer-term goals and needs.

IRSG (Internet Research Steering Group)   A body that is responsible for the coordination of activities within the IETF.

ISO (International Standards Organization)   A standards organization responsible for defining standards for computing.

MAC (Media Access Control)   The MAC layer represents later two of the OSI layers of networking.

MFC (Microsoft Foundation Classes)   A set of reusable C++ classes for Microsoft Windows that were developed by Microsoft.

MIB (Management Information Base)   The database of managed information used by SNMP agents.

MIB II   Management Information Base version II.

MIF (Management Information File)   The database of managed information used by DMI agents.

NOS (Network Operating System)   NOSs typically operate on file servers and offer a variety of services to clients.

NMS (Network Management Station)   A system responsible for management of a network or network subsystem.

OID (Object Identifier)   A variable identifier used to reference an SNMP variable.

OOP (Object-Oriented Programming)   A way of computer programming that views a programming problem in terms of objects and methods.

OSI (Open Systems Interconnection)   An international standard used to allow computers of different manufacturers to communicate with each other.

PDU (Protocol Data Unit)   The basic element of information exchange used within SNMP.

RFC (Request For Comment)   The document format used within the IETF for publishing standards.

RMON (Remote Monitoring MIB)   An SNMP MIB used for performance monitoring of networks.

SNMP (Simple Network Management Protocol)   A standardized IETF protocol used for network management.

SGMP (Simple Gateway Monitoring Protocol)   An early predecessor to SNMP.

SMI (Structure of Management Information)   A set of rules defined in ASN.1 for management information used within SNMP.

TCP/IP (Transport Control Protocol/Internet Protocol)   The network protocol used within the Internet Standards of protocol for network communication.

VB (Variable Binding)   A VB is the associated of an SNMP OID and a variable.

QOS (Quality Of Service)   A term used to describe the quality of services provided by a network.

WAN (Wide Area Network)   A network that spans a wide geographical area.

WinSock (MS-Windows Sockets)   An API used in the MS-Windows environment for Internet protocols.

WinSNMP (MS-Windows SNMP)   An API used in the MS-Windows environment for the SNMP protocol.

WWW (World Wide Web)   A network spanning the world that utilizes the Hyper Text Transfer Protocol (HTTP).

References

[Banker, Mellquist]
Banker, Kim, and Peter E. Mellquist, "SNMP++," *Connexions*, The Interoperability Report, Volume 9, No. 3, March 1995.

[CMIP]
Black, U., *OSI: A Model for Computer Communication Standards*, Prentice Hall, 1991.

[Comer]
Comer, Douglas E., *Internetworking with TCP/IP, Principles, Protocols and Architecture*, Volume I, Prentice Hall, 1991.

[Dataquest]
A Gartner Group Comany, "1996 Network Integration and Support Market Forecast," NISS-NA-MT-9601, 1996.

[Gama]
Gama, Erich, Richard Helm, Ralph Johnson, and John Vlissides, *Design Patterns*, Addison-Wesley Publishing Company, 1995.

[Meyers]
Meyers, Scott, *Effective C++*, Addison-Wesley Publishing Company, 1994.

[Petzold]
Petzold, Charles, *Programming MS-Windows*, Microsoft Press, 1992.

[Rose]
Rose, Marshall T., *The Simple Book (Revised Second Edition)*, Prentice Hall PTR, 1996.

[Saks]
Saks, Dan, *C++ Programming Guidelines*, Thomas Plum & Dan Saks, 1992.

[Stallings]
Stallings, William, *SNMP, SNMPv2 and CMIP: The Practical Guide to Network Management Standards*, Addison-Wesley Publishing Company, 1993.

[Stroustrup]
Stroustrup, Bjarne, *The C++ Programming Language*, Edition 2, Addison-Wesley Publishing Company, 1991.

[DMTF]
Desktop Management Task Force, *http://www.dtf.org*

[Rumbaugh]
Rumbaugh, James, *Object-Oriented Modeling and Design*, Prentice Hall, 1991.

[Steedman]
Steedman, Douglas, *Abstract Syntax Notation One (ASN.1): The Tutorial and Reference*. Isleworth, Middlesex, United Kingdom: Technology and Appraisals, 1993.

[WinSNMP]
WinSNMP, Windows SNMP, *An Open Interface for Programming Network Management Application under Microsoft Windows*. Version 1.1.

[SNMP RFCs]
Internet Engineering Task Force, *http://www.ietf.org*

[WinSockets]
WinSockets, Windows Sockets, *An Open Interface for Network Programming under Microsoft Windows*.

Index

Limited End User Software License
V 2.0

THIS IS A LEGAL AGREEMENT BETWEEN YOU AND FTP SOFTWARE, INC. ("FTP"). READ THESE TERMS AND CONDITIONS BEFORE OPENING THE MEDIA PACKAGE AND/OR INSTALLING THE PRODUCT. IF YOU DO NOT AGREE WITH THEM, YOU SHOULD PROMPTLY RETURN THE PRODUCT TO FTP OR YOUR VENDOR AND YOUR MONEY FOR THE PRODUCT WILL BE REFUNDED.

1. **License Grant:**

    1.1 FTP grants you, subject to the terms and conditions of this Agreement, a royalty-free, personal, non-transferable, non-exclusive license to use the Product as follows:

    1.2 YOU MAY: (a) use the Product internally; (b) physically transfer the Product from one computer to another provided that the Product is used on only one computer at a time and that you remove any copies of the Product from the computer from which the Product is being transferred; and (c) make copies of the Product solely for purposes of backup. The copyright notice must be reproduced and included on a label on any backup copy.

    1.3 YOU MAY NOT: (a) use the Product, except as provided above, (b) copy the documentation portion of the Product, (c) distribute copies of the Product to others; (d) rent, lease or otherwise transfer your rights to the Product; (e) translate, reverse engineer, decompile or disassemble, or otherwise alter the Product (except to the extent described below); or (f) distribute (directly or indirectly) any copies of the Product, or any direct product thereof, to any entity, country or destination prohibited by the United States Government.

2. **Ownership of Product:** The Product is owned by FTP and/or its suppliers and is protected by United States copyright laws and international treaty provisions. It is an express condition of this Agreement that title to, ownership of and all rights in and to patents, copyrights, trade secrets and any other intellectual property rights in the Product, and any copy or part thereof, shall remain in FTP and/or FTP's suppliers.

3. **Support:** FTP shall have no support obligations for the Product.

4. **Term:** This Agreement remains effective until terminated. You may terminate it at any time by destroying the Product together with all copies of the Product in any form. This Agreement shall also automatically terminate without notice if you fail to comply with any term or condition of this Agreement. Upon any termination for any reason, you shall promptly destroy the Product and all copies or portions thereof in any form.

5. **No Warranty:** The Software is provided "AS IS". FTP MAKES NO WARRANTIES, EXPRESS OR IMPLIED, WITH RESPECT TO THE PRODUCT, ITS MERCHANTABILITY OR ITS FITNESS FOR A PARTICULAR PURPOSE.

6. **Limitation of Liability:** IN NO EVENT SHALL THE LIABILITY OF FTP EXCEED THE GREATER OF ONE THOUSAND DOLLARS ($1,000) OR THE AMOUNT PAID FOR THE PRODUCT GIVING RISE TO THE CLAIM. COMPANY SHALL NOT USE THE PRODUCT IN ANY CASE WHERE SIGNIFICANT DAMAGE OR INJURY TO PERSON, PROPERTY OR BUSINESS MAY OCCUR IF ANY ERROR OCCURS. COMPANY EXPRESSLY ASSUME ALL RISK FOR SUCH USE. IN NO EVENT SHALL FTP BE LIABLE FOR DIRECT, INDIRECT, INCIDENTAL OR CONSEQUENTIAL

DAMAGES, INCLUDING, WITHOUT LIMITATION, LOSS OF INCOME, DATA, USE OR INFORMATION, ARISING FROM BREACH OF WARRANTY, BREACH OF CONTRACT, NEGLIGENCE OR ANY OTHER LEGAL THEORY, EVEN IF FTP HAS BEEN ADVISED OF THE POSSIBILITY OF SUCH DAMAGES. Except for any claims by FTP related to FTP's and/or its supplier's intellectual property rights, any suit or other legal action relating in any way to this Agreement or to the Product must be officially filed or officially commenced no later than one (1) year after COMPANY's receipt of the Product.

7. **Infringement Indemnity:** In the event the Product infringes a valid United States patent or copyright, FTP will, provided you discontinue all use of the Product, at FTP's option and expense, (a) procure for you the right to continue using such Product, (b) replace or modify the Product so it becomes non-infringing, or (c) refund the license fee for the infringing Product prorated on a straight line basis over five (5) years. FTP shall have no liability for any claim based upon (a) the combination, operation, or use of the Product with equipment, data or software not furnished by FTP if such infringement could have been avoided through the use of other equipment, data, or software or by the avoidance of use with other equipment, software or data not provided by FTP, (b) modifications to the Product not made by FTP or made by FTP in compliance with your designs, specifications or instructions, or (c) a version of the Product other than the currently released version. This section sets forth FTP's entire liability and sole obligation and your exclusive remedy in the event of any claim of intellectual property infringement.

8. **U.S. Government Restricted Rights:** Distribution and use of the Product and derivative works thereof to and by the United States Government are subject to the RESTRICTED RIGHTS set forth in subparagraph (c)(1)(ii) of the Rights in Technical Data and Computer Software clause at DFAR 252.227-7013. Product described or referenced in this Agreement are commercial computer software programs developed at private expense. Use, duplication or disclosure by the U.S. Government is subject to restrictions as set forth in FAR 52.227-19 (c)(2), the applicable provisions of the DoD FAR supplement 252.227-7013 subdivision (a)(15) or (a)(17) or similar regulations of other United States Federal agencies.

General Terms: The validity, interpretation, construction and performance of this Agreement shall be governed and construed by the laws of the Commonwealth of Massachusetts, U.S.A. Suit with respect to this Agreement may be brought only in the Commonwealth of Massachusetts, U.S.A. English shall be the governing language of this Agreement. If you have any questions concerning this Agreement, you may contact FTP at: FTP Software, Inc., 100 Brickstone Square, 5th Floor, Andover, Massachusetts 01810, U.S.A.

IN WITNESS WHERE, the parties hereto have caused this Agreement to be executed by their duly authorized representatives as of the date set forth above.

LICENSE AGREEMENT AND LIMITED WARRANTY

READ THE FOLLOWING TERMS AND CONDITIONS CAREFULLY BEFORE OPENING THIS SOFTWARE PACKAGE. THIS LEGAL DOCUMENT IS AN AGREEMENT BETWEEN YOU AND PRENTICE-HALL, INC. (THE "COMPANY"). BY OPENING THIS SEALED SOFTWARE PACKAGE, YOU ARE AGREEING TO BE BOUND BY THESE TERMS AND CONDITIONS. IF YOU DO NOT AGREE WITH THESE TERMS AND CONDITIONS, DO NOT OPEN THE SOFTWARE PACKAGE. PROMPTLY RETURN THE UNOPENED SOFTWARE PACKAGE AND ALL ACCOMPANYING ITEMS TO THE PLACE YOU OBTAINED THEM FOR A FULL REFUND OF ANY SUMS YOU HAVE PAID.

1. **GRANT OF LICENSE:** In consideration of your payment of the license fee, which is part of the price you paid for this product, and your agreement to abide by the terms and conditions of this Agreement, the Company grants to you a nonexclusive right to use and display the copy of the enclosed software program (hereinafter the "SOFTWARE") on a single computer (i.e., with a single CPU) at a single location so long as you comply with the terms of this Agreement. The Company reserves all rights not expressly granted to you under this Agreement.

2. **OWNERSHIP OF SOFTWARE:** You own only the magnetic or physical media (the enclosed disks) on which the SOFTWARE is recorded or fixed, but the Company retains all the rights, title, and ownership to the SOFTWARE recorded on the original disk copy(ies) and all subsequent copies of the SOFTWARE, regardless of the form or media on which the original or other copies may exist. This license is not a sale of the original SOFTWARE or any copy to you.

3. **COPY RESTRICTIONS:** This SOFTWARE and the accompanying printed materials and user manual (the "Documentation") are the subject of copyright. You may not copy the Documentation or the SOFTWARE, except that you may make a single copy of the SOFTWARE for backup or archival purposes only. You may be held legally responsible for any copying or copyright infringement which is caused or encouraged by your failure to abide by the terms of this restriction.

4. **USE RESTRICTIONS:** You may not network the SOFTWARE or otherwise use it on more than one computer or computer terminal at the same time. You may physically transfer the SOFTWARE from one computer to another provided that the SOFTWARE is used on only one computer at a time. You may not distribute copies of the SOFTWARE or Documentation to others. You may not reverse engineer, disassemble, decompile, modify, adapt, translate, or create derivative works based on the SOFTWARE or the Documentation without the prior written consent of the Company.

5. **TRANSFER RESTRICTIONS:** The enclosed SOFTWARE is licensed only to you and may not be transferred to any one else without the prior written consent of the Company. Any unauthorized transfer of the SOFTWARE shall result in the immediate termination of this Agreement.

6. **TERMINATION:** This license is effective until terminated. This license will terminate automatically without notice from the Company and become null and void if you fail to comply with any provisions or limitations of this license. Upon termination, you shall destroy the Documentation and all copies of the SOFTWARE. All provisions of this Agreement as to warranties, limitation of liability, remedies or damages, and our ownership rights shall survive termination.

7. **MISCELLANEOUS:** This Agreement shall be construed in accordance with the laws of the United States of America and the State of New York and shall benefit the Company, its affiliates, and assignees.

8. **LIMITED WARRANTY AND DISCLAIMER OF WARRANTY:** The Company warrants that the SOFTWARE, when properly used in accordance with the Documentation, will operate in substantial conformity with the description of the SOFTWARE set forth in the Documentation. The Company does not warrant that the

SOFTWARE will meet your requirements or that the operation of the SOFTWARE will be uninterrupted or error-free. The Company warrants that the media on which the SOFTWARE is delivered shall be free from defects in materials and workmanship under normal use for a period of thirty (30) days from the date of your purchase. Your only remedy and the Company's only obligation under these limited warranties is, at the Company's option, return of the warranted item for a refund of any amounts paid by you or replacement of the item. Any replacement of SOFTWARE or media under the warranties shall not extend the original warranty period. The limited warranty set forth above shall not apply to any SOFTWARE which the Company determines in good faith has been subject to misuse, neglect, improper installation, repair, alteration, or damage by you. EXCEPT FOR THE EXPRESSED WARRANTIES SET FORTH ABOVE, THE COMPANY DISCLAIMS ALL WARRANTIES, EXPRESS OR IMPLIED, INCLUDING WITHOUT LIMITATION, THE IMPLIED WARRANTIES OF MERCHANTABILITY AND FITNESS FOR A PARTICULAR PURPOSE. EXCEPT FOR THE EXPRESS WARRANTY SET FORTH ABOVE, THE COMPANY DOES NOT WARRANT, GUARANTEE, OR MAKE ANY REPRESENTATION REGARDING THE USE OR THE RESULTS OF THE USE OF THE SOFTWARE IN TERMS OF ITS CORRECTNESS, ACCURACY, RELIABILITY, CURRENTNESS, OR OTHERWISE.

IN NO EVENT, SHALL THE COMPANY OR ITS EMPLOYEES, AGENTS, SUPPLIERS, OR CONTRACTORS BE LIABLE FOR ANY INCIDENTAL, INDIRECT, SPECIAL, OR CONSEQUENTIAL DAMAGES ARISING OUT OF OR IN CONNECTION WITH THE LICENSE GRANTED UNDER THIS AGREEMENT, OR FOR LOSS OF USE, LOSS OF DATA, LOSS OF INCOME OR PROFIT, OR OTHER LOSSES, SUSTAINED AS A RESULT OF INJURY TO ANY PERSON, OR LOSS OF OR DAMAGE TO PROPERTY, OR CLAIMS OF THIRD PARTIES, EVEN IF THE COMPANY OR AN AUTHORIZED REPRESENTATIVE OF THE COMPANY HAS BEEN ADVISED OF THE POSSIBILITY OF SUCH DAMAGES. IN NO EVENT SHALL LIABILITY OF THE COMPANY FOR DAMAGES WITH RESPECT TO THE SOFTWARE EXCEED THE AMOUNTS ACTUALLY PAID BY YOU, IF ANY, FOR THE SOFTWARE.

SOME JURISDICTIONS DO NOT ALLOW THE LIMITATION OF IMPLIED WARRANTIES OR LIABILITY FOR INCIDENTAL, INDIRECT, SPECIAL, OR CONSEQUENTIAL DAMAGES, SO THE ABOVE LIMITATIONS MAY NOT ALWAYS APPLY. THE WARRANTIES IN THIS AGREEMENT GIVE YOU SPECIFIC LEGAL RIGHTS AND YOU MAY ALSO HAVE OTHER RIGHTS WHICH VARY IN ACCORDANCE WITH LOCAL LAW.

ACKNOWLEDGMENT
YOU ACKNOWLEDGE THAT YOU HAVE READ THIS AGREEMENT, UNDERSTAND IT, AND AGREE TO BE BOUND BY ITS TERMS AND CONDITIONS. YOU ALSO AGREE THAT THIS AGREEMENT IS THE COMPLETE AND EXCLUSIVE STATEMENT OF THE AGREEMENT BETWEEN YOU AND THE COMPANY AND SUPERSEDES ALL PROPOSALS OR PRIOR AGREEMENTS, ORAL, OR WRITTEN, AND ANY OTHER COMMUNICATIONS BETWEEN YOU AND THE COMPANY OR ANY REPRESENTATIVE OF THE COMPANY RELATING TO THE SUBJECT MATTER OF THIS AGREEMENT.

Should you have any questions concerning this Agreement or if you wish to contact the Company for any reason, please contact in writing at the address below.

Robin Short
Prentice Hall PTR
One Lake Street
Upper Saddle River, New Jersey 07458